PRAYER STILL MOVES MOUNTAINS

Also by Diane Pestes

Prayer That Moves Mountains

PRAYER STILL MOVES MOUNTAINS

DIANE PESTES

Pacific Press® Publishing Association
Nampa, Idaho | www.pacificpress.com

Cover design: Emily Bowen
Cover image: Gettyimages.com
Interior design: Aaron Troia

Copyright © 2022 by Pacific Press® Publishing Association
Printed in the United States of America
All rights reserved

The author assumes full responsibility for the accuracy of all facts and quotations as cited in this book.

Unless otherwise indicated, all Scripture quotations are from THE HOLY BIBLE, NEW INTERNATIONAL VERSION®. Copyright © 1973, 1978, 1984, 2011 by Biblica, Inc.® Used by permission. All rights reserved worldwide.

Scripture quotations marked KJV are from the King James Version.

Scripture marked TLB is taken from *The Living Bible* copyright © 1971 by Tyndale House Foundation. Used by permission of Tyndale House Publishers Inc., Carol Stream, Illinois 60188. All rights reserved.

Scripture marked NKJV is taken from the New King James Version®. Copyright © 1982 by Thomas Nelson. Used by permission. All rights reserved.

Scripture quotations marked NLT are taken from the Holy Bible, New Living Translation, copyright © 1996, 2004, 2007, 2013, 2015 by Tyndale House Foundation. Used by permission of Tyndale House Publishers, Inc., Carol Stream, Illinois 60188. All rights reserved.

Purchase additional copies of this book by calling toll-free 1-800-765-6955 or by visiting AdventistBookCenter.com.

Library of Congress Cataloging-in-Publication Data

Names: Pestes, Diane, 1964- author.
Title: Prayer still moves mountains / Diane Pestes.
Description: Nampa, Idaho : Pacific Press Publishing Association, 2022. |
  Summary: "Prayer draws us closer to God and enhances our spiritual
  growth"— Provided by publisher.
Identifiers: LCCN 2022027456 | ISBN 9780816368600 (paperback) |
  ISBN 9780816368617 (ebook)
Subjects: LCSH: Prayer—Christianity.
Classification: LCC BV210.3 .P4534 2022 | DDC 248.3/2—dc23/eng/20220708
LC record available at https://lccn.loc.gov/2022027456

July 2022

Dedication

To my heavenly Father:
Thank You for the eternal life that is soon to come,
and also for being with me now.
Thank You for promises that display your goodness.
"The fear of the Lord is the beginning of wisdom,
and knowledge of the Holy One is understanding"
(Proverbs 9:10).

Contents

Acknowledgments	9
Introduction	11
Chapter 1: Is the Door Open or Closed?	13
Chapter 2: The One Who Calls You Is Faithful	21
Chapter 3: He Hears Their Cry and Saves Them	31
Chapter 4: A Road of Grace	41
Chapter 5: Even Animals Need Grace	49
Chapter 6: I Am With You Always	60
Chapter 7: So Many Ways God Helps Us	69
Chapter 8: With Us in the Wait	80
Chapter 9: Just How Much Anger Is Enough?	89
Chapter 10: Where Do We Find Our Identity?	99
Chapter 11: The Journey of God's Goodness	108
Chapter 12: Crowding Out the "Bad" with the "Good"	121
Chapter 13: Something That Lasts	130
Chapter 14: Forward With Urgency	141
Chapter 15: Called to Pray	152
Chapter 16: Prayer Still Moves Mountains	163

Acknowledgments

What a blessing it is to have special people in our lives—God is so good!

Special thanks to the following:

Corleen Johnson, my dear friend. I am blessed by the ways our prayers have a big impact on life experiences, and I'm glad we can include some in this book. Thank you for taking the time to read the manuscript through and make suggestions.

My husband, Ron, and my mom, for their love and support. I enjoy experiencing life together—you both are a blessing in my life. Thanks also for being willing to share your life experiences in the book.

My dear prayer partners for their prayers, friendship, love, and support: Corleen, Georgia, Kathy, and Linda.

My friend Georgia Shaffer for her friendship, prayers, and "sounding board" advice.

My friend Bev Schultz for her friendship, shared adventures for God, and example of caring for all she meets.

And family and friends too numerous to mention—they also fill the following pages with incredible, faith-building, life-changing, inspirational, and encouraging stories. We are praising God for many answers to prayer.

Introduction

*The L**ORD** detests the way of the wicked,
but he loves those who pursue righteousness.*
—Proverbs 15:9

It is tempting to peek at the ending of a book to see how a story turns out. While chaos unfolds around me, I sometimes do that with the book of Revelation to encourage myself that we will make it through trying times. Yet living in chaos is where "God moments" still happen. One reason we experience them is because God loves to get our attention. Another reason could be He chooses to respond when we reach out to Him for help.

It's important that we pay attention to God's hand in our lives and through actual short stories. *Prayer Still Moves Mountains* encourages the reader that God loves to respond to our prayers, still does miracles, uses angels to touch people, and waits with us for eternity.

As I write this introduction, it is a windy and rainy day in November. Eleven months ago, in January, I heard my nephew was depressed and lacked direction. In response, I called a few friends and asked them to pray for him with me. He's a miracle baby who was delivered by C-section at the last minute when it was discovered that the umbilical cord was wrapped around his head twice. The medical team said he likely would have died by regular delivery. I have prayed for him throughout his life, and I believe that God has special plans for his life.

Recently, my nephew asked if he could move into my mom's house

[margin note: He's prepping a miracle.]

Prayer Still Moves Mountains

with his girlfriend because after they had moved out of my brother's house they couldn't sustain work to support an apartment. His life feels a little chaotic as he moves from here to there and tries job after job. Yet God reminds us in Proverbs 16:9, "In their hearts humans plan their course, but the Lord establishes their steps." After they moved in, my mom and I prayed for them together. One day, as we continued to pray for them, I saw some type of music player on a table and felt compelled to pray for a thirst for Christian music to grow in my nephew's heart. The next day we heard that his girlfriend had been at an interview and she received a job offer!

I don't know what all God has in store, but I am eager to see what God does, and I am encouraged to see a change in just this short amount of time. God so loves His people and responds when we reach out for help. We pray for people one by one as God puts them in our lives, and we don't know what all goes on behind the scenes. When I pray, I trust that something will come of it.

Meanwhile the world is quickly unraveling and descending into chaos as many people seem angrier and more determined to destroy things. However, I'm encouraged when I look at what happens when we pray. Although I'm convinced God can work without our prayers, I know more things happen because of them. And since I love a good "God moment," it is fun to be involved in prayer-warrior type ways and record what happens. I stand in awe of all He can do—patiently piecing together the pieces of our lives.

May God bless us as we get ready for our heavenly home.

Chapter 1

Is the Door Open or Closed?

> *"I am the L*ORD *your God,*
> *who teaches you what is best for you,*
> *who directs you in the way you should go."*
> —Isaiah 48:17

What should I do next, I wondered. It had been a few months since my friend, Linda, and I had gone on a mission trip to the Dominican Republic, and I needed something else to do. After my morning prayers on June 17, 2011, I called my friend Lois to chat about it.

"Lois, should I wait for an invitation for ministry, or try to find a door where I think God might be calling me?" I asked.

Lois replied, "I think you should knock on doors and continue to pray for confirmation or redirection."

"You know," I responded, "I remember when I was working with Women's Ministries at the Oregon Conference, and Corleen Johnson shared she felt impressed that women needed to do an evangelistic series and then she acted on it. She learned of three places that needed help and chose one that she sensed God indicated would be the best. Likewise, every year Dan Serns plans an evangelistic trip. This past year he asked his daughter Danesa to choose where to go, and she chose the Dominican Republic, which is how Linda and I ended up going there. But what should I do next?"

I didn't have long to wait—the very next day was pivotal. I was at

Prayer Still Moves Mountains

home reading my Bible in Psalms when I looked down at the study notes that read, "The brevity of life is a theme throughout the books of Psalms, Proverbs, and Ecclesiastes. . . . Life is short no matter how long we live. If there is something important we want to do, we must not put it off for a better day. Ask yourself if I only had six months to live, what would I do?"[1] It seemed as though God was really asking me the question and expecting an answer. So I said aloud, "I would do an evangelistic series again."

Well, then what are you waiting for? He seemed to ask.

I prayed, then felt impressed to call Corleen to mention what just happened. I shared the story, then added, "I would really like to go somewhere warm and close, like Arizona. Don't you have a friend that lives there?"

"Yes," she replied.

"What is the name of his church? Maybe that's a place to start." We prayed, and I called the church pastor where her friend attended. After he said hello, I shared that I had just been reading my Bible and the study notes say that life is short and then ask what we would do if we only had six months to live. I shared my passion for doing evangelistic series and wondered if his church had a need.

"My church is already doing a series, and the conference pays eighty percent of the cost, which leaves our church with $4,500.00. Of that, we have raised only $1,500.00. So we can't afford another," he said.

"I was thinking of this as a mission trip and not something where I have to be paid," I responded.

He furthered, "Well there are still costs like advertising. How would you pay for that?"

Suddenly I remembered what we did in Madras, Oregon. "My friend Corleen and I put on an event in a community park in Madras, Oregon. Fifty volunteers came, the church members helped, and a school brought their kids and helped us hand out door-to-door advertising. We gave away a free meal to the neighborhood kids, and many, many, kids came and brought their parents."

The pastor responded, "I do have another church in a small

Is the Door Open or Closed?

community where maybe that type of advertising would work. Would you write up a proposal and email it to me?"

"Sure, I'll do that." He gave me his email and we said goodbye. This was a new dilemma, how do I write a proposal? Then I remembered Corleen had promised she would be praying during my conversation and was eager to hear what happened.

Reaching for the phone, I called Corleen. "You will never guess what happened!" I shared the conversation I'd had with the pastor, and we prayed again with thanks and asked God how to write a proposal. After some research on the internet, I prayed, wrote a proposal, and sent it.

That same day I read Psalm 50, and these three promises seemed to leap off the page at me:

- "For every animal of the forest is mine, and the cattle on a thousand hills" (verse 10).
- "Call on me in the day of trouble; and I will deliver you, and you will honor me" (verse 15).
- "Those who sacrifice thank offerings honor me, and to the blameless I will show my salvation" (verse 23).

God's impressions

As I thought about God's provision in the past, a memory suddenly came back to me. The year before, our friends Lewie and Linda had been with my husband, Ron, and me in that very Arizona town. When we had stopped for gas, I had felt an overwhelming impression to pray for the town, so I said a prayer out loud. Now here I was sending a proposal to serve in that same town.

Providentially, Ron and I already had made plans to go to Arizona in a month. When I mentioned our travel plans in an email to the pastor, the church decided to have their church board meet us and talk about potential plans. A month later, as I sat in front of the small church board and after prayer and greetings, I related, "I'm not here to promote any specific plans, I'm here to see how I can help you."

Prayer Still Moves Mountains

The board members replied, "Every evangelistic series we have ever done has been a flop. However, we have only used videos. We have never had an actual person."

I pondered and replied, "What have you done that has been successful for your church and how can I help with that?"

They responded, "The most successful thing we have done was a cooking school two years ago."

"Great," I answered, "my friend Linda has run cooking schools more than twenty years. If you would like, I can ask her for more information."

"How long could you stay?" they replied.

The proposal to hold a cooking school was voted and approved, and I called Linda on the car ride home. She confirmed that the idea sounded interesting, and we decided to move forward if God kept guiding the plan, then we prayed together.

About a month later, on August 22, 2011, the small-town church was to have a meeting, and I decided to go for a walk and pray about it.

Two days later, a man phoned my house and said, "I'm from the little town in Arizona and just happen to be up here visiting relatives. Can my wife and I come over?"

"Sure," I replied.

Soon they were sitting in our living room. After some small chit chat, the man said, "I'm going to be the new Personal Ministries leader in a couple months, and I've decided my church isn't big enough to handle a cooking school and we won't be ready. How would you even know how to do this in our town?"

I replied, "Every day we ask for God's guidance and go forward trusting that God will open the right doors."

He wasn't satisfied with my response, and concluded, "I'm going to go back and share with the board that this won't work in our town." We had a prayer and he left.

A few months later I learned that they had decided against the idea. Slam went the door on the cooking school for that small town.

Is the Door Open or Closed?

Closed doors and open doors

I've often been reminded that after a door closes we shouldn't stare at the closed door longingly. So after the door closed on the cooking school plan I tried to involve myself in other things.

Have you ever experienced a closed door? Genesis 29 shares the following story:

> Now Laban had two daughters; the name of the older was Leah, and the name of the younger was Rachel. Leah had weak eyes, but Rachel had a lovely figure and was beautiful. Jacob was in love with Rachel and said, "I'll work for you seven years in return for your younger daughter Rachel."
>
> Laban said, "It's better that I give her to you than to some other man. Stay here with me." So Jacob served seven years to get Rachel" (verses 16–20).

We're familiar with the story. A wedding took place, and Laban tricked Jacob and gave him Leah. Jacob was furious. After making a new deal with Laban, Jacob also married Rachel a week later. Just a few verses shed a great deal of light on how this threesome progressed:

- "When the LORD saw that Leah was not loved, he enabled her to conceive, but Rachel remained childless" (verse 31).
- "Leah became pregnant and gave birth to a son" (verse 32).
- "She conceived again" (verse 33).
- "Again she conceived" (verse 34).
- "She conceived again" (verse 35).

Finally, Genesis 30 shares,

> When Rachel saw that she was not bearing Jacob any children, she became jealous of her sister. So she said to Jacob, "Give me children, or I'll die!"
>
> Jacob became angry with her and said, "Am I in the place

of God, who has kept you from having children?" (verses 1, 2).

All Rachel could see was a closed door.

Opening doors

I am reminded of an example of opening doors. In 2008, my friend Corleen and I were in Madras before the "Hope in the Park" event we'd planned, and I said, "You know, I bet we could knock on six doors and find someone who wants people to pray with them."

"You're on," Corleen replied. "I'll come with you, but you have to be the one that gives the invitation."

At the first door no one was home. The second door opened, and I said, "Hi, I'm Diane and this is my friend Corleen. We're from the Madras Seventh-day Adventist Church, and we want to know if you have any prayer requests we could pray with you about."

The woman replied, "That's really nice, but I have a prayer group where I turn in my requests," and made haste to close the door.

At the third door, they mentioned they were Catholic and not interested and closed the door. That was three closed doors so far. As we approached the fourth house we saw a man outside standing on a ladder, so we walked toward him. In response to my comments and question, he said, "My mother is not home, but I'm sure she would like you to pray with her. She likes things like that. Could you come back?"

Yes! an open-door invitation, I thought.

We prayed with people at the fifth house—another open door.

At the sixth house the people spoke Spanish. With my limited understanding of Spanish, I ascertained that their father, who spoke English, would be home at three and we could come back then. They definitely wanted prayer.

Wow, three open doors out of six! For every closed door there was an open one! Truly, God can and will open doors for us.

Is the Door Open or Closed?

If God closes one door

Four months later, in January 2012, an interesting thing happened. One of the members of the small town was discouraged. He had been excited about the cooking school plan but then after another vote, the church decided not to proceed. Soon he felt impressed to dial a friend at another church. He shared that they had passed on the idea of a cooking school and maybe the other church should do it.

Eventually, the Sierra Vista Seventh-day Adventist Church called me to say they were interested in our cooking-school idea. They would offer free lodging and pay for all costs involved with the program. What a huge contrast! Linda and I needed a car to drive while we were there, so we decided to make a road trip out of it and drive instead of fly.

Let's look again at Rachel, who experienced many closed doors. Meanwhile Leah was being blessed over and over again with open doors, but she still didn't feel loved. By Genesis 30, Leah had six sons and a daughter (verses 19, 21), and Rachel remained barren. Verse 22 describes the start of Rachel's new joy, "Then God remembered Rachel; he listened to her and enabled her to conceive. She became pregnant and gave birth to a son and said, 'God has taken away my disgrace.' She named him Joseph, and said, 'May the LORD add to me another son.' " It is often said that good things come to those who wait, and I have found that God will open the right door for us when we obey Him.

Using our talents for ministry

My ministry passions are people, prayer, memorizing Scripture, and sharing "God moment" stories in presentations. Cooking events would be lower on my list, but God makes life more interesting when we are willing to use any talents in ministry for Him. Our cooking school was great fun and a very fulfilling experience.

On May 24, 2011, after reading the story of Esther, I was impressed to write this down in my journal from the study notes, "God has a purpose for the situations in which he places us."[2] When Mordecai learned that the Jews were in danger, "he tore his clothes, put on sackcloth and ashes, and went out into the city, wailing loudly and bitterly"

Prayer Still Moves Mountains

(Esther 4:1). Eventually Esther heard about it, sought a conversation with Mordecai, and learned that she needed to be personally involved. He implored, "For if you remain silent at this time, relief and deliverance for the Jews will arise from another place . . . and who knows but that you have come to your royal position for such a time as this?" (verse 14).

It's a choice. Esther didn't have to be involved, but she chose to. And her people were saved. It is one thing to read stories in the Bible and think, *Oh sure, we would be that heroic also*, and another thing to encounter choices in real life. I didn't have to place a call to someone I didn't know. However, because I did the cooking school, many people were overjoyed to learn new health and food principles.

Living day by day knowing God has a purpose for our situations is assuring. All praise to the Lord for what He does!

Reflection

1. Have you ever had a closed door? Do you have one now? Pray and trust God will open a door soon. Consider journaling your story, then you can add the rest later.

2. If you are challenging God to do something new in your life, jot down a few ways God has led in the past. And praise Him for how He will lead in the future.

---

1. *NLT Life Application Study Bible*, 3rd ed. (Carol Stream, IL: Tyndale House, 2019), 864.
2. *NLT Life Application Study Bible*, 773.

Chapter 2

The One Who Calls You Is Faithful

"My food," said Jesus, "is to do the will of him who sent me and to finish his work."

—John 4:34

The previous year Linda and I, along with Ron and another friend, Lewie, had driven to Tucson, so we knew the road to Arizona pretty well. During that trip we stopped at a Safeway supermarket in Fallon, Nevada, because we assumed it would have a bathroom. As we walked toward the bathroom, I suddenly felt compelled to stop. I stopped so abruptly that Linda bumped into me, and she asked, "Why did you stop?"

A female employee rounded the corner and greeted us as she quickly passed by. "Linda, I feel impressed to pray for the woman who just zipped past us. I think she could really use some prayer." We prayed for her but didn't see the woman again in our time at that store.

Fast-forward one year later, September 23, 2012, Linda and I set off for Sierra Vista to lead the cooking school, and we are convinced that God had us encounter the same woman. We had homemade granola bars and apples packed for our breakfast, which we ate on the road, and then we drove for a long stretch, hoping to find a Taco Bell for our dinner. Taco Bell had introduced their veggie bowls that year, and we looked forward to that treat.

We soon found ourselves in the middle of the Nevada desert and in the same Safeway as the year before. We again stopped to use the bathroom, and Linda wanted to get a fruit cup. As we stood in the checkout line with one fruit cup, the cashier asked, "Do you need a spoon?"

"Yes," Linda replied.

"I'll go get you one from the deli," the cashier offered.

"Thank you, but I'll go get it," Linda said and took off.

I waited for her near the entrance, and she was gone so long that I figured she must have befriended someone.

Sure enough, when she approached the entrance, she said enthusiastically, "I just had a great conversation with a woman in the deli." As we walked out to the car and continued driving, Linda shared that she felt impressed to pray for the woman she spoke with at the deli. So we prayed for her as we drove, and the impression grew that this was the same woman we'd prayed for the year before.

I don't think those two encounters were coincidences. We'd thought about flying, but instead decided to drive. And early on in our trip we were given a glimpse of at least one "God moment" from all the long hours of driving. "My food," said Jesus, "is to do the will of him who sent me and to finish his work. Don't you have a saying, 'It's still four months until harvest'? I tell you, open your eyes and look at the fields! They are ripe for harvest" (John 4:34, 35). I hope to learn the rest of that woman's story someday. In fact, I look forward to discovering how God used all of the prayers we shared as we drove during that trip south. I know that prayer makes a difference!

Some prefer heat

On Monday, September 24, while in Lake Havasu City, Arizona, Linda and I sent the following email to our prayer partners and friends:

> Dear prayer partners,
>
> We stopped in Lake Havasu City because it's along the way, and it is beautiful. It was 104 degrees when we arrived, and Linda thinks that is too hot. But the motel had a pool, and I [Diane] was elated.

The One Who Calls You Is Faithful

The past few months as I pondered our upcoming cooking school, I wondered, *Will Linda have this audience tearing up also? When she shares a message or tells a story, she is so heartfelt and personal. Sometimes she has tears in her eyes, and then the audience often cries too.* Yes, I packed the Kleenex in case people need some. Then yesterday it all made sense in my head as I read my Bible. God called us to do a cooking school, and Paul assures us, "The one who calls you is faithful, and he will do it" (1 Thessalonians 5:24). God calls and He will do it! At the moment they say we have a packed house with fifteen on a waiting list.

This reminds me of Jesus Christ's free gift. For brevity's sake, I'll just mention Romans 10:13, "Everyone who calls on the name of the Lord will be saved." I picture a very long table filled with food in heaven, and Revelation 2:7 shares that Jesus "will give [His people] the right to eat from the tree of life, which is in the paradise of God." Now that will be good food! Maybe even healthful chocolate chip cookies! Is the idea of free healthful chocolate chip cookies for eternity too good to be true? We will see.

You may remember a super illustration of grace in 2 Samuel 9. King David bestowed upon Mephibosheth not only eating at his table for life, but he also returned to him the land, crops, and servants that had belonged to his grandfather, Saul. What a blessing to discover, like Mephibosheth, that there is room for you at the King's table—no waiting list required. Thanks for prayers for our journey!

Diane and Linda

Almost time

As I drove, Linda talked about what she was going to say each night. She'd ask, "How does this sound?" And then she'd share a concept. Then she'd ask, "And which of these ideas sounds better?" *Oh my*, I thought, *these are good ideas. I hope I remember all this because I would*

Prayer Still Moves Mountains

usually be writing all these points down to be used later.

After arriving in Tucson, we went to Whole Foods and Sprouts, and I inquired if we could get several workers to help us with finding items on our list. It was a good thing, because we only had a limited time to shop for a lot of food! That night, we had the orientation meeting and supper with the church members. It was a great way to mingle and discuss the plans. What a great group of people! They had maxed out their table space and budget for the cooking school.

After the orientation meeting, they told us, "Now we have twenty-eight more people who want to come!"

"Since we have a limited budget, if the extra people want to come, they could just sit in for the lectures and not do any sampling," Linda replied.

The church person encouraged, "For now, let's hold to the budget amount. And in order to get the most benefit for the community, we are going to let only church members be involved in the kitchen and not attend the sessions." This was very helpful to maximize the space for those in the community who wanted to come. In the end, it was decided that church members could learn the recipes and watch presentations from the kitchen.

Cooking school

After leading many cooking schools, Linda has a well-thought-out plan for doing them. In Sierra Vista, we set up the cooking school for three nights a week for two weeks: Sunday, Tuesday, and Thursday. Prior to each class, Linda and I organized ingredients; and when the church members arrived, they would prepare the recipe for the evening. The food was then set on a table, like a family dinner setting, in the church's Better Living Center. As church members worked on their food item, Linda would answer any questions the church members had for preparing the recipe. Meanwhile, she also set up cafeteria-like trays to use for explaining how to make one or more of the food items. At 7:00 P.M. the community members would arrive and after prayer get a plate to sample the food. Twenty minutes later Linda made a presentation about

The One Who Calls You Is Faithful

the recipes they had been eating. She also shared about the vitamins they contain and why they are important to the body. Then I carried in the tray with items for the food demonstration, and Linda would demonstrate how to make some of the examples the people had been eating. Next Linda announced we would have a giveaway and I carried in a box of names. The very first night we had a surprise.

"I hope I win!" a woman hollered out from the third row. "This cooking school is just what I needed because I just had a heart attack." With one hand on the top of the box and one hand on the bottom, I lifted the lid to draw out a name and a slip of paper fluttered out. I bent over to grab it and read the name, "Kathy."

The woman who had just shouted burst into tears and made her way to the front. She finally managed to say, "I'm Kathy, and this is so encouraging. Like God is telling me I'm in the right place."

We gave her a book, and Linda encouraged her, "Kathy, this will be a great place for healing." What a blessed start to our cooking school!

Mission with Jesus is not without conflict

Every day I emailed a few prayer partners and friends an update so they could be praying for God's help. In one letter, I explained:

> Your prayers are a continued value to God's success through us, thanks so much. When we first arrived in this town, we saw at least 40 border patrol agents on the main road. An hour after we passed through, they closed the road down for a funeral. Another one has died while we have been here.
>
> Several of the people in the cooking school have mentioned that they are amazed we came so far and took time from our lives to help them. A few have actually shed tears, yes, I'm serious. They also share this time of year was a perfect time for them. People are making decisions about eating better. Some said their doctor had told them they needed to be vegan, and they didn't know where to start. They are also beginning to mention topics about Christianity. Pray

Prayer Still Moves Mountains

for the most important thing—decisions for Jesus. Linda has described the Daniel diet and how that influenced his relationship with God.

One man engaged Linda in controversy about some Biblical topic every time he saw her outside of the cooking school venue. She finally confronted him and asked him to present his arguments from the Bible and he stopped challenging her.

Many times, I've been reminded of the verse that assures us, "A person standing alone can be attacked and defeated, but two can stand back-to-back and conquer" (Ecclesiastes 4:12, NLT).

A government blimp called Aerostat permanently hangs in the air over us for surveillance of the Mexican border. Think we are being watched? We are. Then again, so are you. Hebrews 12:1 shares, "Therefore since we are surrounded by such a great cloud of witnesses."

And they have witnessed so much. They even witnessed the most important event—Jesus hanging, dying, and bleeding on the cross. He didn't get to escape the insults, the rebukes, the punishment, the spiritual warfare. How much does God love you? He stretched out His hands and died. That's how much—His life for yours.

Think we are being watched? We are, you are, by the entire universe to see what our decision for Jesus will be. There is no reason to delay. As the angels reminded the disciples, " 'Men of Galilee,' they said, 'why do you stand here looking into the sky? This same Jesus, who has been taken from you into heaven, will come back in the same way you have seen him go into heaven' " (Acts 1:11).

Joyfully serving out of love, and eager for His return,
                Diane & Linda

In another letter, we shared:

The One Who Calls You Is Faithful

Dear prayer partners,

Linda preaches Sabbath and asks that you pray that Jesus speaks though her very clearly. As I read in my Bible the other day, God gave me this verse in Ezekiel 41:18, "Palm trees alternated with cherubim." That's us down here picturing God's angels among the palm trees.

We had a blessing happen as the church team came up with a plan to get at least ten more people into the class and then someone donated funds for that. If you were reading between the lines, and prayed for those who were waiting, thank you. Now we have about eighteen still on the wait list. I'm glad we could get more in, but I still feel a little bad.

Diane and Linda

Our new friend, Kathy

A few times while readying items in the kitchen before the church helpers arrived, Kathy, the lady who'd had the recent heart attack, came to see us. Her husband also came, and we would sit in the Better Living Center and chat. Kathy asked many questions about health principles and recipes. She wished that we could stay longer—or at least promise to come back! She and Linda figured out that they both owned dogs that were boxers and were delighted they also had that in common. They exchanged phone numbers and at the time of this writing are still calling one another. They studied the books of Daniel and Revelation over the phone with another friend, and they plan to continue studying the Bible together. A few years later, Linda and I, along with our husbands and my mom, were even able to make a trip to visit Kathy at her lovely home. It is so nice to make friends here for eternity!

Sous chef

Just call me a "sous chef," or "the top assistant in a professional kitchen."[1] It would not be my passion to be a professional chef; however, I have some allergies that make learning healthy, tasty recipes necessary. Learning to cook whole-food, plant-based meals is better with fun recipes and makes it easier to accommodate my needs.

I remember one day when we went shopping for the ingredients for the next night. We were in the produce section, and Linda, searching for various produce, requested, "Can you grab an onion?" I walked to the onions and took two and came back to the cart. "We only need one," she said.

"As I reached out for one though, I felt compelled to get two," I replied.

"We are on a budget, and the recipe only calls for one," she said.

"I'm keeping track of the budget, and I think we can afford an extra," I replied.

Two days later, I began to work on a recipe that called for the one onion. Because I was unfamiliar with a chopper that someone had brought for us to use, the onion was whizzed into liquid. It was definitely not supposed to be liquid. Thankfully we had another onion to use instead!

We had a great variety for our six nights, each night a different theme: breakfasts, picnic foods, Italian, holidays, soups, and recipes for food intolerances.

God is holding us

One Sabbath, Linda and I received directions to a trail along the San Pedro River from a local, who said, "I know a good hiking trail by the river." So we set out. What seemed like a long way down the road, I asked, "Can you see where this road ends?"

Linda looked at the map and replied, "It ends in Mexico." I practically stomped on the car brakes because I remembered years prior going into Tijuana from San Diego, and there was no warning we had actually crossed the border. Thankfully, moments later we found the road into the park. We enjoyed exploring the trail, and even got to watch a group catching and examining hummingbirds. At first, I thought it was really cute, but soon I started wondering how the bird felt. Surely the bird wouldn't like going through this experience, and

The One Who Calls You Is Faithful

I wondered what purpose it would serve. But there was a reason for their momentary discomfort.

In a similar way, God corrects and encourages our growth and sanctification. Rather like Job 5:17, "Blessed is the one whom God corrects; so do not despise the discipline of the Almighty." Just as Rachel learned trust, dependence, and patience, I have learned that God is the one holding us in His capable hands. And He can open a door when one shuts, and in His timing.

Please don't go home

At the end of our two weeks of cooking classes, many people came up one by one and shared how much weight they had lost in just two weeks, one lost ten pounds, another eight, yet another six. One woman held up her arms for me to see skin sagging where it had been filled out before. There were many testimonies about how lives were changed. People lost weight, and they were going to share the information with their family and friends.

"When are you coming back?" many asked us.

Another said, "You can stay at my home, and I will cook for you."

One adventurous woman wanted to take the drive back to Oregon with us and then fly home!

Linda and I choked up with emotion as we listened.

Our new friend, Kathy, lingered the longest. She had a special prayer over us and then hugged us before we left.

Now I have a mental picture when I read about Paul's farewell to a group from Ephesus, "They all wept as they embraced him and kissed him. What grieved them most was his statement that they would never see his face again. Then they accompanied him to the ship" (Acts 20:37, 38). Won't heaven be wonderful? No more goodbyes!

This experience taught me that when I am called by God, I need to go, and "the one who calls you is faithful" (1 Thessalonians 5:24). And it will all be worth it!

Here are two more verses of encouragement for our journeys whether we stay near home or go farther abroad. Paul wrote, "But thanks be to

Prayer Still Moves Mountains

God, who always leads us as captives in Christ's triumphal procession and uses us to spread the aroma of the knowledge of him everywhere" (2 Corinthians 2:14). And Jesus shared, "He will always give you all you need from day to day if you will make the Kingdom of God your primary concern" (Luke 12:31, TLB).

Reflection

1. Journal about a time you were so focused and excited about mission that the mission was more important than the food on the journey. Or take a moment to pray about your next opportunity to reach people for Christ.

2. Share about a time when it felt as though God was stretching and growing your faith, or correcting you.

3. Would you like to share with God that you want to make the kingdom of God your primary concern?

---

1. *Merriam-Webster.com*, s. v. "sous-chef," accessed April 4, 2022, https://www.merriam-webster.com/dictionary/sous-chef.

Chapter 3

He Hears Their Cry and Saves Them

The LORD is near to all who call on him,
to all who call on him in truth.
He fulfills the desires of those who fear him;
he hears their cry and saves them.
—Psalm 145:18, 19

While Linda and I were in Tucson, we visited a woman who wanted prayer. In the course of our visit, we asked her, "How long have you had this heart condition?"

She replied, "Several years, and because of it, I've had to give up my favorite game—golf. I just don't have the energy anymore. Please tell me about your cooking school."

So Linda and I shared some stories and details about the cooking school. Then we had a prayer with her before we had to leave.

That morning, my quick note to our prayer partners had been, "Linda and I are very sleep deprived. When the recent nonstop schedule ends, we may fall asleep for a week. Oh, and Linda is dehydrated. Trying to drink more hasn't helped so far. Thus, prayers for sleep and water would be appreciated. It is interesting that God, with His sense of humor and timing, led us to Galatians 6:9 this morning, 'Let us not become weary in doing good.' Blessings to you all, Diane & Linda"

We were very thankful for all who were praying for us as we traveled home. In our next prayer email, Sunday, October 14, 2012, I shared,

Prayer Still Moves Mountains

As we traveled across California today toward the ocean, Linda was driving on a long, straight stretch of road. We saw a long line of traffic coming toward us in the other lane. The third car back pulled out into our lane and came toward us, and I thought, *What are they doing? There isn't room!* Sure enough, as they came closer, they suddenly realized we were there just as Linda turned into the shoulder. They saw they would hit us and also pulled to our same shoulder. We bore down on each other in the shoulder lane. Traffic behind us continued in our lane so we couldn't pull back in. We finally stopped twenty-five feet from that car with traffic roaring by. My heart was pounding. Even though this cooking school is over, we aren't home yet, and prayers for continued safety would be appreciated. Last night we were in Cambria, where we stayed at a very delightful place with a pool. This morning we had a buffet breakfast without feeling rushed—we feel relaxed and refreshed.

God is good. We aim to be home Wednesday. I want to thank you so much for your prayers on this journey. This has been an incredible trip with many God moments, and lots of people who now wish to, and know how to, eat healthier.

Blessings and love, Diane and Linda

It's hard to part
Linda's husband, George, picked her up along the way, and I headed home. It's hard to part after an experience of doing something together for the Lord. It was Wednesday, October 17, 2012, and as I read my Bible that evening, God reminded me of these verses as if in confirmation and affirmation of all He had done on the mission trip, "I will tell of the kindnesses of the Lord, the deeds for which he is to be praised, according to all the Lord has done for us—yes, the many good things he has done . . . according to his compassion and many kindnesses" (Isaiah 63:7). Also Jeremiah 31:16, "This is what the Lord says: 'Restrain your voice from weeping and your eyes from tears, for

He Hears Their Cry and Saves Them

your work will be rewarded,' declares the LORD." It felt as if we had been crying out in prayer to God about this trip for a long time, and now it was done.

The first thing each morning I usually pray, "Lord, fill me with Your Holy Spirit power to be in the right place at the right time with the right information in my hands and the right people in my path." Sometimes I still wonder what I will be doing next, but when I look back, I can see that "God moments" have happened.

Clackamas Town Center mall shooting

It was Tuesday, a day that I usually volunteer at the chaplain's office. But this week they had asked me to switch to Wednesday. It was December 11, 2012, and Ron and I decided to meet my mom for a late lunch at the Clackamas Town Center. As Ron and I arrived in the parking lot, I was overcome by a sense of dread and the certainty that I needed to pray for the mall and especially the Macy's store. As we walked toward the restaurant, we saw my mom drive up. She didn't find a close parking spot and had to drive around. Earlier she had mentioned that she was going to Macy's afterward. Again, it felt as though I was supposed to pray for her protection too, so I did. As we left after lunch, she went to walk through Macy's and lingered looking at items. Afterward she said, "I walked out to my car and checked the time. It was three o'clock."

Tragically, at 3:28 P.M. a gunman entered the mall and opened fire. He killed two people, severely injured a third, and then killed himself. "Roberts fired only seventeen rounds during the entire shooting, including the one to kill himself. An additional 128 rounds were found in the magazines he dropped and on his person."[1] The authorities closed the mall down soon after the shots rang out, and many people were locked down as officers investigated and cleared the mall.

How providential that God nudged me to pray in advance that day—only in eternity will we see what all was prevented or helped as a result of this prayer. As for my mother, God answered my prayers for her, and she left before the shooting began. I am so glad I cried out to

Prayer Still Moves Mountains

the Lord ahead of the chaos, and I can't help but wonder what other "God moments" occurred that day.

The Lord is also near to us
Looking back, I am always amazed at how much God's people have to go through before we get to our heavenly home. My mom was taking care of my dad, who had Alzheimer's, and she just dashed out to get her hair cut but tripped on a curb walking toward the hair place, breaking her wrist. It was December 13, two days after the mall shooting. She waited till after her haircut to phone me, "I think I broke my wrist. It is misshapen, but I can probably drive home."

"What! How did you do that? Where are you? Don't move. I'll come get you," I urged.

"No, I think I can drive home. Then my car will be at my home," she responded.

"I think I should come get you," I said.

"No, I can make it home," she assured me.

"All right, I will meet you at your house and then take you to the doctor," I stated.

My thoughts began to race: *Now that Mom needs care, who will take care of Dad? I'm so thankful for our caregiver, Mark's, help during the day, but what about at night? How bad is her arm hurt, and is it fixable?* I sent up more prayers, crying out to God. It pains me so much to watch people suffer.

The doctor gave Mom Vicodin for her pain after doing the X-ray. Later, we received a call from the doctor: "A radiologist looked at the X-rays and said the bones are crushed to one side and there is a fracture of a bone. She won't be able to see the surgeon until Monday, and then we should know more."

I called my paramedic friend, Lewie, and he assured, "Diane, they often make people wait for any surgery until the swelling goes down."

This made me feel better since her wrist was very swollen. *What if those prayers I felt compelled to pray on Tuesday for my mom's protection at the mall were for now too*, I wondered. *Wow, if this happens when we*

He Hears Their Cry and Saves Them

pray, what would happen if we didn't? I am thankful for such promises as Psalm 94:22, "But the LORD has become my fortress, and my God the rock in whom I take refuge."

On December 16, I sent Georgia an email:

> Update on my mom: Her hand and wrist have turned a blackish-grey in color and both are swollen. I head to my house each afternoon for several hours to see Ron and my dog. I've told my mom that I can have one of my friends stop by while I'm gone, but each time she refuses help. She can't use her left hand, and yesterday she admitted to doing too much while I was gone. So far, in addition to watching her and my dad, to occupy time and amuse myself, I have installed more shelves in the pantry and thrown out past-dated items. She likes the new shelves because they have created more space.
>
> Days later, while my mom was in recovery from surgery, I felt compelled to run an errand. Upon my return, as I walked toward the hospital entrance, I saw a lady limping, and I asked, "May I help you?"
>
> She responded, "Not unless you can heal me." Acts 3:6 flashed through my mind, "Then Peter said, 'Silver or gold I do not have, but what I do have I give you. In the name of Jesus Christ of Nazareth, walk.' "
>
> I responded to her, "Well, I could pray."
>
> And she was very appreciative that I did.
>
> My mom had four pins put in her arm, and we are staying at my home for a few days. We need to get a bed for her downstairs so we won't bother her when we are taking care of my dad while she recovers. Diane

Again, I am thankful for such promises as the one in Psalm 145:18, 19, "The LORD is near to all who call on him, to all who call on him in truth. He fulfills the desires of those who fear him; he hears their cry and saves them."

Prayer Still Moves Mountains

I find it helpful to remember that when I help with the simple things God sets before me, I'm doing the important work. How wonderful to know that the Lord is truly near to us.

Snatched from the fire

While wondering what to do next, have you ever felt vulnerable, unprotected, or unsure that you're making a difference? In the book of Zechariah, we see how much he worked to reassure the people. One day to encourage Zechariah, God gave him a vision of Joshua, the high priest for the remnant who had returned to Jerusalem to rebuild. In his capacity as high priest, Joshua represented the people before God. Zechariah 3:1 shares, "Then he showed me Joshua the high priest standing before the angel of the Lord, and Satan standing at his right side to accuse him."

Paul states in Romans, "As it is written: There is none righteous, no not one" (Romans 3:10, NKJV). Satan stands beside us to accuse us because he knows our sins. However, the Lord answers for us. Zechariah 3:2 shares, "The Lord said to Satan, 'The Lord rebuke you, Satan! The Lord, who has chosen Jerusalem, rebuke you! Is not this man a burning stick snatched from the fire?'"

I'm so thankful that the Lord comes in, rebukes Satan, and describes us as a stick snatched out of the fire. As a young child, John Wesley was in a house fire. His family escaped the fire, but in the rush to leave his family forgot him. As they looked back at the house, they saw John was standing at the upstairs window. People quickly stood on shoulders and broke the window to get him out. As a result, his mother Susanna Wesley called him a brand snatched from the fire.

I find it interesting that as an adult John Wesley struggled with his faith. He witnessed to a thief once and wondered how the thief could accept Jesus so simply and quickly when he himself couldn't. However, he continued to meet with his brother Charles once a week to study the Scriptures and pray with others. This is one of the early reasons they were called Methodist, because of the methodical way they carried out their Christian faith. Then one day his brother Charles invited him to a

He Hears Their Cry and Saves Them

meeting at Aldersgate to hear someone new, and John went along.

When John Wesley heard the preacher's words, "Faith is God's work in us," his heart was strangely warmed. He stood up and said, "Now I know that I never could have worked out my own salvation. It is a gift of the most high God. My friends, that great gift is mine tonight."[2]

That night, John accepted the gift of God's love. "This resulted in a long and vigorous ministry including field preaching, training of lay preachers, establishment of (Methodist) societies and schools, medical clinics and publishing books and tracts. His vital preaching challenged the complacency of the established church."[3]

John preached faith. One day he received a letter from George Whitefield, who was preaching to coal miners and people in the fields near Bristol. George wanted to sail for America to preach there and wanted John to take his place in Bristol. John went to have a look and told his friend he had earlier thought that trying to reach people outside a church was a sin, but as he looked over the people milling about, his heart went out to them as Jesus' had when He was on earth (see Matthew 14:14).

John's journal records his feelings about sharing Jesus with full vitality.

> God in Scripture commands me, according to my power, to instruct the ignorant, reform the wicked, confirm the virtuous. Man forbids me to do this in another's parish; that is, in effect, to do it at all, seeing I have now no parish of my own, nor probably ever shall. Whom then shall I hear, God or man?
>
> I look upon all the world as my parish; thus far I mean, that, in whatever part of it I am, I judge it meet, right, and my bounden duty to declare unto all that are willing to hear, the glad tidings of salvation.[4]

Perhaps he referred to Romans 11:29, "For God's gifts and his call are irrevocable."

Prayer Still Moves Mountains

John built meeting houses for people to get together and worship, and he also preached to people in fields wherever they were. Usually John would try to frequent all his churches and preach at them. But he also gathered and exhorted lay ministers in their visitations to "pray with the people, rejoice with them, where necessary reprove them, do all you can to turn them back to God."[5]

We also can be ministers

I like the thought that we are a brand plucked from the fire and God holds us in His hand and places His mark where it needs to go. A mark is rather like God's seal. Second Corinthians 1:22 puts it this way, He "set his seal of ownership on us." Like Wesley, we too have a similar urgency. In the name Seventh-day Adventist, the word *Adventist* represents that we are looking for Jesus' soon return. We, too, look for opportunities to pray with people, rejoice with them, where necessary reprove them, and do all we can to turn them back to God. We are witnesses, declaring praises, whether our audience is one or one hundred. Whether we are running a cooking school or helping someone who has a broken wrist. Peter wrote, "But you are a chosen people, a royal priesthood, a holy nation, God's special possession, that you may declare the praises of him who called you out of darkness into his wonderful light" (1 Peter 2:9).

We do this as we visit people, give Bible studies, pray with people, and have intentional conversations. God will help us to be witnesses for Him. To tell others about Jesus gives us great eternal joy. I really like the assurance of God's provision recorded in Luke 12:31, "He will always give you all you need from day to day if you will make the Kingdom of God your primary concern" (TLB).

Let's go back to Zechariah 3:3, 4, "Now Joshua was dressed in filthy clothes as he stood before the angel. The angel said to those who were standing before him, 'Take off his filthy clothes.' Then he said to Joshua, 'See, I have taken your sin, and I will put fine garments on you.' " I really like this visual of Christ washing away our sins with His own blood—He gives us His robe of righteousness.

We heard about how John Wesley made a mark. We, too, are making

He Hears Their Cry and Saves Them

a mark because the other end of the brand is held in our Maker's hand. It is as if we are helping stamp the name of Jesus everywhere. God has made us pure so we don't have to feel vulnerable, unprotected, or unsure that we are making a difference. God is using us to make His mark. Zechariah watched this happen in a vision. Zechariah recorded, "Then I said, 'Put a clean turban on his head.' So they put a clean turban on his head and clothed him, while the angel of the Lord stood by" (Zechariah 3:5). We have Christ's righteousness on us as we go about our duties, and we may ask ourselves how it feels to have Christ's robe covering our sins.

We don't need to wonder what we will do next, or "become weary in doing good." Our loving God goes before us and will help us in ministry for Him. He hears our cry, uses our efforts, and saves us and others because we shared Jesus.

Reflection

1. What type of things do you do each morning for worship with God, before starting your day? If you have "aha moments," are you recording your insights or Scripture promises in a journal?

2. Think through who you might call if you need help. Call that person in advance of any issues and tell them you think of them as someone you can count on in an emergency. Then ask if you can call them in an emergency.

3. Further research for Christ's righteousness can be found in 2 Corinthians 5:21, Ephesians 4:24, and Revelation 19:8.

4. Review the story in Zechariah 3 about how God combats the enemy for us. How does this make you feel? Journal a time God guided your talents (ministry) for Him.

Prayer Still Moves Mountains

1. Mark Spross, "Mall Shooting Clackamas Town Center," Archive.org, September 11, 2013

2. *John Wesley: The Faith That Sparked the Methodist Movement,* directed by Robert Fernandez (Worcester, PA: Vision Video, 2013).

3. *John Wesley: The Faith That Sparked the Methodist Movement.*

4. John Wesley, *The Journal of John Wesley* (Grand Rapids, MI: Christian Classics Ethereal Library), 65.

5. *John Wesley: The Faith That Sparked the Methodist Movement.*

Chapter 4

A Road of Grace

*But if we walk in the light, as he is in the light,
we have fellowship with one another, and the blood
of Jesus, his Son, purifies us from all sin.*
—1 John 1:7

I would like to find a house where the sun shines on it and next to a nice road to walk," I said to Ron as we searched for a new place to live. We had spent several years living at the bottom of a hill where the sun didn't shine in the winter and there were only a couple of blocks to walk around in circles. God helped us find a home where the sun shines in the winter and there are three miles of road to walk on nearby! As I began walking on the road and waving at people who waved back, I discovered something even more valuable—a road of genuine, caring people. What a huge blessing this is, both as I reached out to help others and as they have blessed us also. I love these divine appointments, or God moments!

A couple years a neighbor lady hosted a Christmas party in her home for the ladies who lived on the road. This provided a great opportunity to get to know others. She read a Christmas story and said a prayer before we ate some food. I was touched by the atmosphere of grace. Then several years went by and no invitations came. Feeling compelled, I decided to reach out with a Christmas invitation, and I began praying that God would bless my endeavors and the ladies who would come. As I handed an invitation to one of the women, she said, "Thank you.

Prayer Still Moves Mountains

This is nice, and I should be able to come that day. Since we are fairly new to the neighborhood, I have a desire to meet a lady with children that are my kids' age."

"That would be very helpful. I will pray for that too. See you later," I replied and then turned to leave. It took me three days to tape invitations to mailboxes or hand them out to ninety homes. My invitation included my phone number and email.

"Diane, what if too many ladies come? They won't all fit in your house," remarked my friend Sandy, who lives on an adjoining road. I had just explained I had invited every lady on our road to my house for a Christmas potluck and fellowship.

"I'm fairly sure they won't all come. God will guide who needs to come though. Would you be in charge of getting people something to drink when they arrive?" I asked.

"Yes, that sounds fun. I'll bring some hot and cold drinks," she replied.

Soon I received a few responses from those who could come or those that said they would have, but they were doing something else that day. The Sunday afternoon finally arrived, and we had about thirteen ladies arrive with some sort of food item to share. After a little time of sharing in the living room, we sat down at the table to eat some food and then the doorbell rang. It turned out that the latecomer, Julie, who sat down by the lady that needed to meet someone with children her children's same age. It was a "Divine appointment" that they met because now their children are indeed friends too. I love stories where God makes connections happen!

Kelly had cancer

"Do you know my wife, Kelly?" A man called to me from a truck at the edge of the road as I approached. As I walked, I was talking on the phone to my friend Georgia Shaffer when a man pulled his truck up to the edge of the road a little in front of me. He rolled down his window and then called out to me.

"Just a second," I said to Georgia. "A man is calling out to me, and I need to go over to his truck."

A Road of Grace

"Do you know this man?" she asked.

"No, I don't think so," I responded, trying to get off the phone, "but I've got to go. I'll call you back."

"Are you sure this is wise?" she asked.

Feeling compelled with urgency and interest, I responded again, "I've got to go. I'll call you back."

"I'll be praying," she replied.

Now near the truck, I heard the man repeat his question, "Do you know my wife, Kelly?"

"I don't think so." He didn't seem to mind that I didn't know and continued, "My wife, Kelly, was diagnosed with cancer and is starting treatments soon."

"Oh no, I am sorry to hear this," I responded. Wanting to do something, I added, "I will be praying. Would it be alright if I come over in a day or two to visit?"

"Yes, you can," he replied, then drove off. This man had so much love for his wife and was distraught over her ailment, that he shared it with everyone—even strangers on the road. I had never met him or his wife before.

That evening, I called my friend Sandy at the end of the road. "Do you know T. J. and Kelly?" I asked her. She hadn't met them or heard their story but thought she knew where they might live when I described the long driveway where he met me.

"I would like to go with you when you visit them," she replied. I started praying for Kelly, and the thought came to me, *It's nice to take something along when you visit.* A couple days later, I decided to make potato salad to take to T. J. and Kelly, then headed out with Sandy. T. J. met us at the door with his children and sister-in-law. "Hi T. J., we came to see Kelly and pray with her. I made you some potato salad," I said as I held it out.

"How did you know potato salad is one of my favorite foods? My mom used to make a really good one. Now no one ever makes it for me," he said.

"The Holy Spirit must have impressed me. I'm so glad I could bring something you like," I replied. He introduced me to his sister-in-law and the children who had gathered in the entryway. I introduced Sandy. Then he sadly shared, "Kelly is too sick right now to get out of bed and not up for visitors."

"That's all right," I replied. "Would you like for me to have a prayer right here?" We held hands around the circle and I prayed.

Afterward Kelly's sister-in-law mentioned it was a beautiful prayer and asked if I was a chaplain. I replied, "No, I just like to pray for people and have seen wonderful answers through prayer." It was a nice connection that Sandy and I made with this family on the road. And I have maintained the connection. In fact, T. J. went on to tell us that the pizza parlor he works for delivers to Hood View Adventist School once a week. So they were already acquainted with Seventh-day Adventists. A few months later, Kelly stopped her car on the road and thanked me for praying for her. She was doing well, and many months later she stopped again to report she was healed. A couple of years after that I again knocked on their door to share that my first book had been published. T. J. invited me into the house to share with the children while he finished some yard work. One child excitedly ran to get a pet chinchilla for me to hold while we sat in the living room and they told me their "God moment" stories. It is good to meet people on the road that God puts in our path.

It is all about the people

We can't take our possessions with us to heaven, only people. It's all about people: including the people, loving the people, blessing the people, and urging the people. Not expecting anything in return—we just hope to turn them to Jesus. After all, isn't that what Jesus did?

God puts people in our path to love, help, and minister to. But we have a choice—stay on that side of the road and help, or cross over to the other side and ignore them. One day as I was walking home, I saw the woman that some people say is doing drugs. She is very thin from walking everywhere because her boyfriend owns the car, it breaks down, or he doesn't want her to use it that day. A couple of times I have picked her up when I was out driving and saw her walking. As I saw her approaching me, I said, "Hi, Tabitha, how are you?"

"I'm doing fine," she replied.

"Where are you coming from?" I asked.

"I walked to the bus station, and I just got back from selling my plasma. They gave me sixty dollars for that," she responded.

"Really?" I said, my mind grasping at what must be a desperate need for money. I turned to walk in the same direction she was walking and began talking about food. "Before I started walking today, I made some vegetarian burgers. Would you like to have some?" I asked.

"Yes, I would like that. I'm not a vegetarian, but I know it is supposed to be good for you," she responded. We turned around, walked back to my house, and entered my kitchen.

"Ron, this is Tabitha. She lives down the road," I mentioned to him. He greeted her, and they had a conversation while I packaged up some burgers. And then I walked her home.

When I got back home, Ron said, "Did you listen to her? She was higher than a kite and must be on some drug. I can't believe you brought her into our house."

"Yes, but she was hungry," I answered matter-of-factly.

Reaching out

One day while walking, a neighbor greeted me as she was standing by a fruit tree next to the road. "Hi Diane."

"Hi, I'm sorry, but I don't remember your name," I replied as I walked closer.

"Michelle," she responded as she approached.

We started talking, and she asked about the paper I was holding. "Today I am practicing a talk that I am doing soon at a church," I responded.

"Oh, good, you are a Christian," she replied. She shared with me the story of how her husband died of prostate cancer and complications with pneumonia that lingered. The medical team tried to save him but couldn't. Her loss weighed heavily on her heart. After listening to her story, I shared how sorry I was to hear about her loss. I shared that one thing that helps me after a loss is to journal and pray about my pain and sorrow.

I offered to pray with her, and afterward she said, "You know, Diane, I have been feeling God's nudge lately that I should journal, and your words were a confirmation of this for me. Thank you." And then she hugged me.

It's amazing how many opportunities cross my path as I walk on the road near my house. On December 22, 2018, a man driving a truck suddenly lost the trailer he was towing as he drove by me. I jumped out of the way not realizing it was connected to a chain—slowing the trailer down as it dragged along the asphalt. When the trailer came to a loud halt, I paused to let the smoke clear a bit, then I stepped back onto the road and walked around the truck. "Hi, I'm Diane. That was a strange thing to happen. I'm glad the chain held. Could I help somehow?" I asked.

The man replied, "I'm Gary, and I recognize you from your frequent walks along the road."

He looked quite thin, and I thought, *We are not going to be able to lift that trailer onto the hitch.* My brain searched for information, and then I remembered. Earlier in the year, Sandy had mentioned that there was a man in the neighborhood who had cancer. This must be him. I started praying in my mind. *Heavenly Father, please help him with strength. I hope he knows You.*

"We are going to need a jack," he said, interrupting my thoughts.

"I can call my husband, Ron, and ask if he has one," I replied, finding my husband's number on my phone.

"You don't need to do that. I can go to my house and find one," he replied.

"Oh it's no problem. Ron is used to me calling for his help for a variety of things while I'm on my walk," I said. Ron came in a few moments with a jack, and the two of them put the trailer back on the hitch. It's a good feeling to be in the right place at the right time to help someone.

A Road of Grace

Eleven months later, on Sabbath, November 16, 2019, Ron and I walked into church and saw a large table with a whole bunch of rubber bracelets next to the entrance to the sanctuary. Drawn in by curiosity, I picked one up. It read, "Never Alone," then a little blank spacing and also the words, "Called and Loved." *That's really confirming. I like that*, I thought, and put it on my wrist. We heard a nice sermon about the topic and then went home.

Ron and I had been invited to a neighbor's house for the evening. It was an early holiday get-together for all the neighbors. Part way through the evening, a woman named Karen walked in, and I found out that she had just lost her husband to cancer. It soon dawned on me that her husband was the man Ron had helped with the jack on the trailer. Walking over, I said, "I am so sorry to hear you lost your husband."

She shared with me that God had been assuring her that she was never alone. And then a little later she said something about being called by God. That comment really peaked my interest. She added, "My husband didn't go to church or have a relationship with God. It was three days before he died that I suddenly felt impressed to ask Gary if I could call the pastor to come and pray with him, and he said, 'Yes.' Diane, would you believe he gave his life to Jesus and had tears running down his face after the pastor's prayer and touching appeal?"

"Oh Karen, that is so amazing. I am so glad you were impressed to call the pastor." Later in the conversation, I shared the story of receiving the bracelet earlier in the day. "Look at this. It has the words you said earlier—that God had impressed that you are never alone and you are called by God. I want you to have this bracelet to remind you of that." She thanked me and put it on.

About a year later, as I was walking on the road, Karen stopped her car and thrust out her left hand and said, "Look, Diane, I am still wearing the bracelet you gave me as a reminder." God is so good at keeping track of the pieces of our lives year after year. I am very thankful for this and a road of grace-filled people.

Prayer Still Moves Mountains

Reflection

1. What do you do to get to know your neighbors?

2. Have you considered memorizing anything on your walks? Or items to give to the neighbors?

3. Ponder and journal what you might do in advance of someone being hurt on the road in front of you.

Chapter 5

Even Animals Need Grace

*In his hand is the life of every creature
and the breath of all mankind.*

—Job 12:10

Tigger is a vicious pit bull who lives next door to us. When we approach the fence, he tries to attack us, which reminds me to be thankful for strong fences. For safety reasons, we usually walk our dog, Boomer, on a leash. One day we thought the coast was clear as we let Boomer outside without a leash. As Boomer got near the fence, Tigger ran over and tried to bite him. He was ferociously barking and biting through the fence as Boomer yipped and growled back while staying a few inches away from those big teeth. Ron heard the commotion, ran toward the fence, and reached down to pick up Boomer, but Tigger bit Ron on his upper arm through the fence. Boomer slipped away and went further down the fence line, and Ron had to make a flying tackle to get Boomer. A doctor's visit revealed bandages would work and no stitches were needed, but the bite did leave a scar. After that, Ron thought I shouldn't walk on our road, but I assured him that I have a sword via Scripture pages.

Sure enough, a few months later, February 24, 2013, as I walked back to my house, Tigger slipped under the fence and ran at me barking ferociously. My reflexes acted immediately, and I held out my Scripture cards in front of me as protection.

Everywhere he turned, I turned. With the cards held out the whole time, it seemed as if he was stopped by the Scripture cards. His owner came running out into the street calling Tigger, who finally turned to go home. Out of the corner of my eye I saw a man was running toward me with a knife. That seemed odd, but when he reached me, he said, "I saw that dog running at you, and I came with what I had. I was going to poke the dog with my knife. What did you do, hold him off with paper?" he asked.

I explained, and then I waited till I reached my driveway to laugh in relief as the verse in Hebrews 4:12 came to my mind, *"For the word of God is living and powerful, and sharper than any two-edged sword"* (NKJV).

Not all animals are vicious
"How many dogs came out this time?" Ron often asks after I return from a walk. Frequently, a few dogs come to the edge of their yards for the biscuits that I carry. This has been helpful more than once when I tried to catch a stray or a dog who has escaped from its fence.

One time, an unfamiliar, large, and unfriendly looking dog came toward me. I held out a biscuit, and it grabbed the treat from me. Then for a few years the dog came out every time I walked by. It always looked mean as it walked up, took a biscuit, then turned around and walked back home. Thankfully, he just wanted the treat I offered.

One day I saw a dog up ahead that had a beeping noise on him. As I got closer to him, he didn't seem as though he were going to attack or anything. I tried to give him a biscuit and grab his collar. He took a little bite swipe at me and wouldn't take the food. "Ron, come quick with a leash. I need help catching a dog," I said on my phone. The dog kept going down the road darting back and forth aimlessly while I tried to keep up. Ron arrived and made an attempt to put a leash on him but was reluctant. "What if he tries to bite me?" he asked. Ron went back for the truck, and the dog followed him. Ron stooped down, and the dog came as Ron got the leash on him. I called the number on the tag just as a black van drove up and a man jumped out to say the dog was his. I was so glad we detained the dog. Who knows what might

Even Animals Need Grace

have happened if we hadn't with darkness approaching. He might have wandered too far into a yard to spot from the man's van. I'm glad we connected him with his owner.

Our own dog, Boomer, sleeps on our bed for a while before we take him to the laundry room, where he sleeps the rest of the night. But if he starts crying during a storm, we bring him back to our bed to comfort him. Matthew 10:29 asserts that not even a little sparrow falls to the ground without God knowing. And I have some precious pets I hope I will see again in heaven. For this reason, I hope Psalm 36:6 is literal, "Your righteousness is like the highest mountains, your justice like the great deep. You, Lord, preserve both people and animals." Therefore, I imagine God also really cares about the animals out there who are displaced.

One morning shortly after Ron left for a videographer job, I stood in the kitchen with Boomer and looked out at the bird feeder. It looked empty so I took some food out. Suddenly I heard Boomer barking ferociously at the front of the house. He kept barking as I came inside and went to the front door to look. There on the front porch was a German shepherd. Not sure if it was friendly, I decided to open the door a crack. He didn't move, so I brought food and water and set it in front of him. That slowed him enough as he looked down at it that I reached out and grabbed his collar, wanting to see if his collar had a phone number, but he started jumping around. I held on and put him in the garage. Then I called a neighbor, Mac, who was able to hold the dog still as we dialed the number on its tag and left a message. There was also an address on the tag, so I walked to the next street and around the corner and knocked on the door—no one answered. I decided to let the dog have a break in the backyard. He ran around in a frenzy and leaped up the rock wall at the highest part like it was nothing, and I realized, *Oh no this dog could easily jump the fence!* Sure enough, he hopped over the fence, and I ran after him. Next, he put his paws on a wire fence and tried to climb it. Thankfully, he came when I called him, and I breathed a prayer of thanks as I put him back in the garage. More time went by before a woman returned my phone call and then came

Prayer Still Moves Mountains

to get him. Whew! Another dog saved and given back to their owner.

Worth the trip

It was August 2008, and the North Pacific Union Conference (NPUC) Women's Ministries director, Sue Patzer, had organized a NPUC Women's Ministries Retreat at Sea to Alaska. We were to do mission work in several cities as well as some sightseeing. Sue put all of the conference women's ministries directors in charge of something for the evening programs. However, as we approached the departure date, Sue suddenly couldn't go on the cruise and asked if I could coordinate the evening meetings as I saw fit. Thankfully, she was able to fly in and join us for the city of Ketchikan. Each evening I made the announcements. Sue Hess, from Alaska, gave a fact about Alaska each night and found someone to pray. Wilma Bing, from Washington, was asked to be the icebreaker person. Corleen Johnson was asked to lead music. Then a different person each night was doing a women's ministries focus time, followed by a song by Margie Salcedo Rice, and a speaker.

Corleen and I arrived early in Seattle on Sunday to greet the ladies and pass out name tags. Then we boarded the ship and unpacked our carry-on items. I received a call from the travel agent, who suggested I should go meet the person on the ship responsible for setting up our meeting rooms. We went down to first floor and met Peter, who said, "Diane, for some of the meeting times we have another group in the room your group desired. Your group will need to meet in a different room."

"Could we go look at the rooms you are talking about?" I asked. We did, and they were fine. He was very helpful and as the week continued, and we had only a few minor tweaks in the timing of our meetings. Only on Sabbath did we have to meet in a different room—but even this ended up being a blessing because the new room felt more worshipful anyway.

Monday morning I awoke to an ocean-only view outside my window. Curious, I walked to the other side of the boat and it was an all-ocean view there as well. I had never been that far out on the ocean before.

Even Animals Need Grace

Since this was an outreach trip, at three ports of call we would spend part of the day doing mission projects and mingling with the people. By the time we reached Juneau on the third day, I was ready to walk on flat ground. But flat ground was short-lived as the pastor took Corleen and me to the end of town to hand out literature. The literature had a sticker on the back with the name of their church. If you have visited Juneau, you know that at one end of town all the homes are built on stilts. This necessitated a climb up a flight of stairs before I knocked on the door and discovered that most people were not home yet. Then I would place a piece of literature on the door, climb down the stairs, and continue to the next house. After twenty houses I was tired! I looked at our literature and prayed, "Lord, is this doing any good? I pray for the people who receive it that Your Word will not return to You void and it will be a blessing. We want to change lives. Thank You. In Jesus' name, amen."

At the next port of Sitka, Corleen and I and a few others handed out teddy bears to the fire department, fifty baby layette sets to the native hospital, gave a donation of cash to the women's shelter, and checked on other team members who were cleaning bird cages at the bald eagle bird refuge. A woman named Linda drove us around in her car while her husband, who had two broken ankles, stayed in bed at home. It was touching that she took time away from caring for him to help us.

Ketchikan was our last outreach stop, and by this time, I had the thought, *You know, I haven't really had a lot of time to myself just to sightsee in all these places.* I had heard that Ketchikan had a beautiful area with a creek called Creek Street with a row of homes and businesses that hang over the creek, and it was something I really wanted to see. *It would be fun to take a walk on it*, I thought.

When we arrived in Ketchikan, Corleen and I ran off the ship at seven thirty in the morning to see a couple sights before we needed to meet Sue Patzer and start some outreach tasks. At the exit to the ship we ran into someone who had a question, and that delayed us. Then we stopped at a store with wonderful souvenirs and purchased some.

Prayer Still Moves Mountains

By the time we reached the historic Creek Street, I only had time to take two pictures before going to meet Sue. I thought, *I'm not going to get to see Creek Street.* We got into a car with the pastor and dashed to the church to put together gift bags for women who would attend a meeting later. Then we headed toward a senior living facility to help four women who needed help with upkeep and cleaning their homes. Again, I thought, *I'll have to clean a home, dash back to the church for the meeting, and then immediately for the boat. I won't get to see Creek Street.*

Immediately I sensed God reminding me, "Inasmuch as ye have done it unto one of the least of these my brethren, ye have done it unto me" (Matthew 25:40, KJV). God was pointing me to the more important thing—His people. So I walked into the senior center and met Pat. The first thing she said was, "Do you mind making my bed? I can't make it and usually have to wait until a relative comes over. I bought some bright sheets because this place is so dreary."

"Oh sure, I would love to help. Those are very pretty sheets," I responded, thinking, *Wow something so simple can make a big difference.* Ida McCray helped me, and then I glanced at the floor and it was clear that it needed vacuuming. When I was done, I walked across the hall to the room Corleen was cleaning. There I met Dorothy. She was sitting in her pajamas, which didn't really cover her. Her dog sat beside her on the floor. I vacuumed her floor and then suggested, "Dorothy, your dog probably would enjoy a walk outside, may I take him?"

"Yes, that would be great," she replied.

"What is your dog's name?" I asked.

"Precious," she replied.

"That seems fitting," I replied. Meanwhile, Corleen was cleaning up the bathroom floor where Precious had left behind a smelly mess. Precious and I trotted down the hall—Precious was in obvious need of exercise. I wanted to go up the stairs, so I pulled and his neck stretched forward, but he didn't move his legs. I pulled, and he still objected. He kept looking at the fire door, so I thought, *Well, maybe he normally goes through here instead of up the stairs.* We went out the fire door and paced back and forth around the front of the building. These little

Even Animals Need Grace

things are so important, because they are big things to the people God wants to reach. I walked Precious back to his owner. Corleen washed her hands, and we jumped into a taxi to go to the church. We had our meeting, and as we dashed away toward the ship, I couldn't help but think, *I didn't get to see Creek Street.*

I imagined God peering down from heaven and shaking His head as He reminded me, "But you are going to be walking streets of gold soon." That thought made me pause. I knew He was asking me, "How can you even compare a connection with a person or a dog with seeing a unique street?" I can't. People and dogs are more important than earthly sights because we all are going to be walking streets of gold soon. Hallelujah! Amen!

Peanut makes a helpful connection

One February, while working at the Gladstone Park Church, I took bulletins to a couple of ladies who live in the assisted-living facility next door. While delivering the first bulletin, I saw a dog approaching with a woman in a wheelchair behind him. I stooped down to pet the dog, and she said, "Oh, are you a dog lover?"

"What's his name?" I asked.

"Peanut," she replied. Peanut's leash had gotten tangled in the wheels of the chair, and I helped her roll backwards to get it untangled.

"I'm going to go back for my sweater. We are going outside for a walk," she replied and wheeled around. I continued on my way to deliver a bulletin to another lady, and we chatted a few minutes before I took my leave. When I rounded the corner from her room and walked down the corridor, I saw the woman with the dog again. She was getting her mail. Walking toward her, I asked, "Would you like me to walk Peanut for you?"

"You wouldn't steal him, would you?" she replied.

Startled, I responded, "No, I would never do that."

"Are you sure?" she asked.

I assured her that I wouldn't, thinking, *This is her most meaningful possession, no wonder she is worried!*

Prayer Still Moves Mountains

"OK, you can walk him," she answered.

I took him outside for a walk and then brought him back in. As I glanced around, I wondered where she went and thought, *I am really going to be in trouble if I can't find her.* Just then I saw her in a back room talking with a staff member. Walking up to the dog owner, I shared, "Well, it looks like you are busy. I'll walk him in the back for a bit."

When I came back and handed her the dog leash, she asserted, "I don't even know who you are. And here I let you walk my dog."

I replied, "I'm Diane, and I'm the office coordinator at the church next door. It is usually on Thursdays that I come over and bring bulletins to two ladies who can't get over to church anymore."

Just then, the staff lady she had been talking to spoke up, "I have been meaning to call you. We recently had a staff member die while they were on the job. Our other staff members were so upset that they had to be let off for the day. Management had to bring more helpers in. We had a celebration of life service for the residents and staff, but the family members would still like a private service for them. And they didn't have any money to have one. Does your church charge?"

"No, this sounds like something we would be able to do free of charge," I replied, and explained about our facilities with two nice kitchens for various sized crowds. Then I gave her phone numbers to call our event planner. And sure enough, we were able to be a blessing for a family who had a need. As I walked away that day, I thought, *What if I hadn't asked to walk a stranger's dog? I wouldn't have been able to talk to the staff member about her pressing need. Only God can line that up!* And the woman almost didn't let me walk her dog because she didn't know me.

Over the next year and a half she would occasionally bring her dog by so we could walk together. Then came the day when she was no longer able to take care of her dog in her room. She phoned me to ask if I would take in Peanut. He now lives at our house and is the sweetest little dog. God knew in advance that he would need a home, and He provided a home with me. Peanut is now a visual reminder of how God

Even Animals Need Grace

plans for us in advance and provides for our every need.

God wants to rescue dogs—and us too

One dark and rainy October day, while I was driving home from work, I noticed the figure of a big dog in the road darting in and out of traffic ahead of me. *He looks like he is dragging a chain and must be some scary pit-bull type,* I thought. Out loud I said, "Oh Lord, You have to help him. I don't want to stop for a wet pit bull in the dark. Send him back to his own yard. I promise that the next lost dog I see in the road I will rescue." I rolled past the dog feeling a little better. Surely God would put him back in his own yard. I wondered what would happen to me though after making such a promise. After all, when we make promises to the Lord, He remembers.

Two weeks went by, and then one day I again saw a dog in the road up ahead. It was walking along slowly. Slowing down, I watched as a car ahead of me drove past and the dog seemed to look them over then turn back to gaze at the road ahead. I pulled alongside the dog, stopped, and rolled down my window. He walked over, then stood up on his back feet with his front paws bent and did a little hop. It looked like he was begging. Not even thinking that the dog might be dirty, I jumped out, opened the back door, and said, "Get in. You're going home." Surprisingly, he jumped up on the seat. We rounded a couple of corners and drove in the driveway. I put him in the back yard with some water and food. He drank some water but then started pacing the yard frenetic like. *He must be worried and want his real home,* I thought. I felt so bad. I went inside for a chair so I could sit outside and watch him.

As I walked past Ron in the library, I said, "Ron, I had to bring a dog home. He is in the back yard if you want to come take a look."

"We can't house a strange dog. We already have a dog. What if he has some disease and gets our dog infected," Ron responded as he went to look at the dog. "I have seen that dog before when I was driving, about two weeks ago and further away on a different road," Ron said.

"Really? Oh no. That means he has been homeless at least two weeks and no one has rescued him," I replied. I really felt bad for the dog now. "Well Lord, You know where his home is. I need You to help me find it," I said out loud to God.

Outside I watched the dog go back and forth in the yard. He circled closer in his frantic pacing and finally came right to me. I just put my arms around him and started praying again, "Lord, You know where this dog lives, and he needs his real family. Someone must really be missing him. Surely You had this in mind for me to stop this time for a reason. Please comfort him and help him to know he is loved and that I am trying. I know You can do something." I stroked his fur and prayed more.

Later, knowing his family wouldn't appear out of nowhere, I got up and went to my computer. There were two animal shelters in nearby communities. I phoned the Multnomah County Animal Services in Troutdale first. Assured that they would take him that day, I went to fetch him from the yard. I imagined him thinking, *Now where am I going? I hope I am going home.*

Sometimes it feels as though I am constantly uplifting a prayer. It is a good connection feeling like a lifeline. Others don't know all the answers, but God sure knows everything. We all want to have a place to call home where we feel love and acceptance. Surely animals do too. In one of Job's responses to his friends he assures them God has His hand in the life of every creature. Job 12:7–10 states, "But ask the animals, and they will teach you, or the birds in the sky, and they will tell you; or speak to the earth, and it will teach you, or let the fish in the sea inform you. Which of all these does not know that the hand of the Lord has done this? In his hand is the life of every creature and the breath of all mankind."

I prayed out loud for the dog all the way to the shelter. I really wanted this to work. Reaching out for the first person I saw, I said, "I found this dog near where I live and hope you can find his real family. I don't want him to be put down if someone doesn't claim him. I need to know what happens to him." They wrote a number on a card and said it was his number and to call in three days. I could hardly stand

Even Animals Need Grace

it to wait the three days to hear the outcome.

On the third day I was so elated when they said, "His name is Junior, and his family came the very next day to get him. In fact, they had been coming every day to look for him for two weeks because they were so eager to find him." Then it hit me, Junior probably went missing the day I promised God I would pick up the next dog He put in front of me. God is like that. He gets people to pray for us too, in advance of our need. He has been looking for us every day. He's seen us on the road when we were lost and worried. He wants to take us home to our loved ones here on earth, and one day soon to our eternal home as well. Soon. He says in Luke 10:20, "But rejoice that your names are written in heaven."

Reflection

1. Take some time to find other verses of how God cares for animals. Journal about how you would feel if your own pet were lost, and then found. How does it feel to know God is watching you and eager to take you home?

2. Consider sharing an animal story for a school or church children's story. Start by writing it down now. It's also helpful to practice by telling the story to a friend.

Chapter 6

I Am With You Always

"And surely I am with you always, to the very end of the age."
—Matthew 28:20

Suppose you have a goldfish named Bubbles in a bowl that you are keeping on the counter, and every day you flick food into Bubbles's bowl but do nothing else. Several weeks later you notice that Bubbles looks as though he is swimming in dirty water. You pull Bubbles out and wash him off under the faucet with a tiny brush and special fish soap. Then you put Bubbles back in the same water. Pretty soon he is going to get dirty again. Even if you gave him fresh water, pretty soon Bubbles is going to get dirty again. Yes, he has been washed by you the "parent," but Bubbles needs to have some sort of "filter" that works to keep him and his bowl fresh. If we were talking about us, this means we not only get food and drink in the church potluck line but also spend quality time in Bible studies, men or women's fellowship events, and engage in quality conversations. It also means a daily relationship with the God who wants to be with us 24-7. No one else can be with us 24-7.

God wants to be with us always, no matter where we are. He says, "So I will be with you." The idea of God being with us is in many verses. I'll mention a couple. Isaiah 43:2 shares, "When you pass through the waters, I will be with you." And Matthew 28:20 encourages, "And surely I am with you always, to the end of the age."

I Am With You Always

Beginning the process

If our life were described as a picture puzzle, then we could only see a few pieces at a time and we need to trust that God is working to complete the whole puzzle. Joseph was able to view a few pieces in advance, but he didn't know what they meant. God gave him a dream in Genesis 37:7, "We were binding sheaves of grain out in the field when suddenly my sheaf rose and stood upright, while your sheaves gathered around mine and bowed down to it." And another in Genesis 37:9–11:

> Then he had another dream, and he told it to his brothers. "Listen," he said, "I had another dream, and this time the sun and moon and eleven stars were bowing down to me."
>
> When he told his father as well as his brothers, his father rebuked him and said, "What is this dream you had? Will your mother and I and your brothers actually come and bow down to the ground before you?" His brothers were jealous of him, but his father kept the matter in mind.

Joseph learned he really had to trust God because his life suddenly took a turn for the worse as those dreams he shared were the "last straw" in the minds of his brothers and soon they sold him to Ishmaelites. A little later in the story we see the key phrase "The LORD was with," and we are encouraged that we, too, can hold on to the I AM as we go through life. It is in Genesis 39:2–4, "The LORD was with Joseph so that he prospered, and he lived in the house of his Egyptian master. When his master saw that the LORD was with him and that the LORD gave him success in everything he did, Joseph found favor in his eyes and became his attendant. Potiphar put him in charge of his household, and he entrusted to his care everything he owned." Notice that the key phrase is listed twice. What a comfort to know that God is with us as we go about our lives and serve Him.

Several years ago, a woman told me she was going to be training as a medical assistant and that she would have to clean many bedpans,

Prayer Still Moves Mountains

and there is no identity in that. Then she told me, "At least you have an important job."

I said, "Oh no—I don't think of any job as a title. My title is servant of God, and there is more identity in that than anything in the world. Try thinking of yourself as 'servant of God.'"

"You're right. I think I will," she replied.

Dear fellow servants of God, if we know the Lord is with us always, we are emboldened to encourage one another to do whatever our hand finds to do and do it with all our might. We are not always thinking of the next open door but that what we are doing now is just as important as what we might do someday.

Face value

The other day I went to the bank and handed the teller a hundred-dollar bill and two twenties to put in our account. The hundred was a blessing we received for Christmas as a present—we don't have them lying around. The teller took the three bills and placed them in her drawer without any fanfare. Sometimes when I go to certain stores and hand them a twenty, they hold it up to the light, mark it with a pen, and act suspicious, as if I may be giving them counterfeit money. But the teller just gave my money a glance and put it in her drawer. It reminded me of when I worked at a credit union years ago. We took training in looking at money and learned the characteristics of it. We were told: always study the characteristics of genuine money till you know it well—never study fake money. If you study the true, you will recognize the fake instantly. I thought, *This is true spiritually as well.*

Later, I mentioned my bank experience to an older person, and they said, "Have you noticed when you ask for money back at the bank, it comes out of a machine sometimes face up or face down. Yet, before the teller counts it out to me she puts them all face up."

"Yes, I've seen this," I responded.

"Yes, but do you know why?" she asked.

"No, I guess not," I responded.

"Years ago, money was able to be manipulated and bad people would split bills in half. They would take one twenty and cut it in half and paste them onto the back of two ones and pass them off as two twenties. So banks started saying money was only worth the face value and made sure they were face up when they counted them. It became a habit. In fact, if you accidentally tear a bill, in order for it to still have value, you need the picture on the front and three quarters of the bill to turn into the bank for replacement."

In truth, the only blessing we have that is worth more than "face value" is Jesus Christ. Let's invest in Him for eternal blessings.

Time to be refreshed

Personally, I have found a great way to start the day with God. I read a devotional entry, the quarterly Bible lesson study, and the Bible and then pray with God about the day and prayer requests others may have. Many times, I notice that something I read applies to a situation I face later in the day. Another good way to see how God is with us is to take some quiet time away from our regular routine. This is a good "filter" from the storms of life that helps to keep us fresh in our relationship with Jesus.

Sometimes God uses one event to encourage two people. Many years ago, my grandmother was in great tooth pain but lacked money to fix the issue. Thankfully, I was able to find a low-cost dental place near her. As we pulled up and stopped in front of the door, she told me she was anxious, and I took her hand and said, "Then let's have a prayer first." Next, we walked to the counter to check in and then took our seats. Just then a golden lab dog walked around the corner over to her and set his head on her lap as she giggled. He left his head there as though he knew she was anxious and needing soothing. I felt relieved, too, that God helped ease my grandmother's anxiety.

Two deaths

Seventh-day Adventists have a book called *Seventh-day Adventists Believe*. One of the beliefs is called "Growing in Christ." It is a unique principle in any Christian's life that our Christian growth begins with death—two deaths really. There is the belief in the death of Christ on my behalf, and the belief in the death of self. Jesus explains it this way, "For God so loved the world, that he gave his only begotten Son, that whosoever believeth in him should not perish, but have everlasting life" (John 3:16, KJV).

The process of dying to self includes admitting and confessing our sins to God. Proverbs 28:13 says, "Whoever conceals their sins does not prosper, but the one who confesses and renounces them finds mercy." Confessing our sins means that we state what our sins are, we are sorry for them, we are willing to renounce them or give them up, and we are willing to be transformed by God. Then we really should accept forgiveness—because it is a promise. First John 1:9 says, "If we confess our sins, he is faithful and just and will forgive us our sins and purify us from all unrighteousness."

It's amazing that God would give up His Son for us, but it's more amazing that His death was for my sins and yours. The cross is a symbol of God's victory over evil. Colossians 2:13 says it makes forgiveness possible, "You were dead in sins, and your sinful desires were not yet cut away. Then he gave you a share in the very life of Christ, for he forgave all your sins" (TLB).

For example, people may not forgive us for things we have done even if we ask forgiveness, but God always forgives. And God instantly accepts us when we confess our sins. Christ's death was not just for me personally, but it is a universal reconciliation. This is further elaborated in 2 Corinthians 5:19, "That God was reconciling the world to himself in Christ, not counting people's sins against them. And he has committed to us the message of reconciliation." And it urges that point home in the next verses, "We are therefore Christ's ambassadors, as though God were making his appeal through us. We implore you on Christ's behalf: Be reconciled to God" (verses 20, 21).

This passage not only gives us assurance of victory now but also a purpose as an ambassador for Christ.

I Am With You Always

No one should miss the grace of God

Every day I pray that God will use me to help His people, and sometimes His people seem to appear out of nowhere in front of me. Thus I need to be alert that each person I meet is someone God sent. A Scripture passage that guides our attitude toward meeting people is Hebrews 12:14, 15, "Make every effort to live in peace with everyone and to be holy; without holiness no one will see the Lord. See to it that no one falls short of the grace of God."

One night I stopped by the grocery store for onion soup mix. While there, I spotted a man who was unshaven and wearing slippers and sweatpants. He shuffled past me and turned the corner, leaving his cart behind. Thinking to myself, *This seems a little odd*, I continued my shopping. But a few minutes later I saw his cart sitting in the same place. *Where did he go?* I wondered as I looked around. Then I saw him five aisles away. Feeling Holy Spirit compelled, I moved forward. "Are you looking for your cart?" I asked when I reached him.

"Yes," he responded. "I'm not sure where I left it."

"It is five aisles back that way. I'll walk with you," I assured. At that point, I wasn't sure if he had dementia, and I didn't really want to leave him unattended. We reached his cart, and I implored, "Are you going to be OK?"

"Yes, I think so," he responded. Unsure that he would be, I left that aisle again looking for the elusive soup mix. Eventually I gave up and decided maybe I was there for another reason. *Where did he go?* I wondered as I turned around. *Oh there he is standing by himself again without the cart and looking sluggish.*

"May I help you with anything?" I asked.

"I have a real hard time thinking," he replied. "I have pancreatic cancer, and the chemotherapy has been really hard on me. My feet won't lift more than five inches off the ground, and my legs are swollen and feel heavy."

Gasping inward slightly, I expressed, "I'm so sorry you have to go through this."

My mind raced, thinking, *He may not have too much time left, and I*

Prayer Still Moves Mountains

don't want him to die without hope. So I asked, "Are you a Christian?"

"Yes, I am a Christian." Then he shared a little of his faith and expressed that it gave him hope for what was to come.

Maybe the Holy Spirit, in that moment, wanted to remind him of the most important thing we have? Or maybe he needed someone right there in the moment to come along side him because he looked and felt lost? Surely God was right there with him and bent down to hear his words of faith.

As the man paused at what seemed to be the end, I expressed, "I would be happy to pray for you right now if you wish . . ." My voice trailed off as I unexpectedly saw a woman approaching us with the missing cart. She looked friendly as I held out my hand. "Hi, I'm Diane, and I was being helpful. My father had chemotherapy, so I know about the tiredness, but I'm so sorry to hear about the pancreatic cancer."

"My name is Dolores," she responded as she grasped my hand in return. "Thanks for trying to help. It's been hard."

I looked back at the man as he peered tiredly down at his grocery list and then said, "I guess we should be going, we have things we need to do."

"May God bless you," I said in farewell.

We may never know how meaningful our presence is to someone else. Our words, our thoughts, our actions, our prayers for His people are never in vain. God knew that space in time would be there. God knew how much it mattered. God assures me it is worth it in these words I shared earlier, "Make every effort to live in peace with everyone and to be holy; without holiness no one will see the Lord. See to it that no one falls short of the grace of God" (Hebrews 12:14, 15). I'm glad I stayed alert on the grocery man. It blessed me also just to be present in that grocery store, helping and pointing to the One who is with us always.

Fishing for people

Casting is a fishing term. When I was seven years old, my dad took our family fishing. We camped at Trillium Lake, and my father and I joined several others along the lakeshore. As I looked down the line at

I Am With You Always

all the men, I prayed that I would catch a lot of fish. I started pulling in fish and was a little amazed that my prayer worked! At least seven fish were mine, and men came over to ask my dad what type of bait I was using. "We just have worms," he replied. I knew I was praying though and was so impressed that God was answering. It really helped build up my young faith.

Catching fish is not my problem if I have a pole and a worm and I'm doing all the right things, such as casting the worm in the water. What was I doing differently? I was praying in the faith of a child, "O God, I need You to help me." Oh wait! I still use that line. And He really does. Now that I'm older, I've learned that "casting" for people for Jesus is really just using the talents God has given me for His honor and glory.

Dogs are good examples
Awhile back, we had a beloved pet dog named Tornado. He loved to walk around our outer fence line and then return to the house. I didn't realize how much he relied on the fence line until he started showing signs of blindness. One day I watched him from the window when he strayed away from the fence line. He got out into the field and then turned in circles like he was trying to find his way back to the fence line. I realized he was lost and went out to get him. When I picked him up, he totally relaxed in my arms and sighed, as if he was saying, "Oooh, what a relief, my mom has found me." I have never forgotten that illustration, knowing, *God watches me also and picks me up in His loving arms when I am lost or disheartened.*

God is with us to the end
During the fall of 2016, my mother-in-law couldn't keep track of her pill schedule anymore ,and we signed her up with a visiting angel service to stay with her every morning for two hours. They give her pills, make sure she eats breakfast, and on Sabbath, they drive her to church. Joan,* her visiting angel and now friend, was assigned to take

---
* Joan is a pseudonym

Prayer Still Moves Mountains

her to church and had quite the experience because she didn't have a church of her own or know God personally. It wasn't long before she revealed to me that she felt she was being ministered to there and it felt like her church. Her husband and son started coming with her. She took Bible studies for a while with one lady and then studied with another lady. Tara became her very good friend.

Joan's son, age ten, commented one day, "Mom, before Ruth, we didn't have Jesus in our home. Ruth gave us Jesus." Several months later, Joan was baptized, and her Bible study friend Tara read Joan's testimony. It was heartwarming and refreshing that she had endeared herself to the church and vice versa.

God used my mother-in-law, who needed help herself, to shine His love to everyone she meets. Daily, God is with her, making connections happen to refresh others.

Do we want to be refreshed and know that God is with us? Remember, Jesus loves us. We can focus on Jesus and what He has done, deny self, and walk the new life. Let's not miss an opportunity to pray or connect with others. Let's live the new life. It is good for us to be here with Jesus. He is with us always.

Reflection

1. The Lord was with Joseph. Take a few moments to cite some other places in the Bible where the Lord was with people. And perhaps write down a time in your life when you know the Lord was with you and how that gives you courage that He still is with you.

2. What are some ways you have taken God at face value? For example, how do you relate to John 3:16 and 1 John 1:9?

3. Ask someone if you can share with them about a time when God has encouraged you and let you know He was with you. Maybe they would like to share a time with you also.

Chapter 7

So Many Ways God Helps Us

The righteous cry out, and the LORD hears them;
he delivers them from all their troubles.
—Psalm 34:17

"I don't think we have enough gas to get there," I observed to Ron.

Checking Google maps on his phone, he replied, "It says we have 101 miles to reach Beatty, Nevada."

"Yes, but the car says we only have 151 miles before we are out of gas," I replied.

"That should be enough," he said.

We had driven from Bryce Canyon National Park and were now headed to Death Valley National Park but planned to stop and stay overnight in Beatty, Nevada. We had become more interested in National Parks when my mom started a list of how many she had seen, and we decided to help her add to the list—Death Valley would be park number eighteen for her.

We finally arrived in Beatty, Nevada. The next morning, we discovered that Denny's is a good breakfast spot in the tiny town. Then again, it was the only option that didn't look rundown. I was enticed by the Fit Fare Veggie Sizzlin' Skillet—I hoped it would hold me for a long time. After all, there are not many food options in Death Valley!

Arriving at Death Valley, we were astounded by the vastness of the valley floor with mountains on either side. About the middle of our journey through we stopped at the Furnace Creek Visitor Center and

Prayer Still Moves Mountains

posed for pictures. As we neared the very popular Badwater Basin, known for being 282 feet below sea level and the lowest point in North America, we saw that the parking lot was full. We could see people hiking way out on the salt flats. "Oh look, that car just pulled out. We can take that one," I said as I pulled in. Mom and I got out of the car and started down the walkway a few feet when I turned back to notice that Ron stood near the window of the car next to us. He had noticed two young ladies sitting in the car next to us, and the driver held a cold drink can to her forehead. He then tapped on her window and indicated for her to roll it down. When she did, he asked, "Do you have a headache? I have aspirin if you need it."

"Yes," she replied.

Immediately, Ron was aware that he had a problem. He knew it was a terrible idea to offer medication to a stranger. And someone should never accept medication from a stranger. Yet he realized he needed to do something. He went back and got the aspirin from the car. He wanted to be accurate and to put her at ease. At her window he said, "This is an over-the-counter pain reliever called Vanquish. It contains acetaminophen, aspirin, and some caffeine. The adult dosage is one or two tablets every six hours." He handed her two tablets and then urged, "Take it with lots of water."

Her friend leaned over from the passenger seat and thanked Ron profusely.

Later, as we were out hiking on the salt flats, Ron asked, "Do you think that was meant to be?"

"Oh yes! All the spots were full and that car pulled out at just the right time. Then we pulled in right next to the person who needed help. I think God set it up for you to help that lady. We were surely at the right place at the right time. It is a great example of how God helps other people through us," I responded.

Another time, we were visiting eastern Oregon with four friends and planned to hike at Todd Lake and kayak at Elk Lake. Our friend, Ed, noticed that a storm was coming sometime and suggested, "Maybe we should go to Todd Lake first because everyone is going to be walking and not everyone will be kayaking. Then if the storm comes in, we can forgo kayaking." We all agreed and went to walk around Todd Lake first. It is a lovely lake with a trail near the water's edge the whole way around and Mt. Bachelor in view for part of the hike. The storm hadn't hit yet, so we decided to kayak. Since we had four kayaks but six people, Ron and Sandy stayed behind. Thirty minutes later, as he sat in the truck overlooking the lake, Ron saw a flashing out in the water. Then he recognized that a canoe had tipped over and the people were in the cold water trying to right it. They tried three times and failed. It didn't look good, and Ron ran to the small lodge and called for help. A lodge employee immediately ran and jumped into a large fishing boat and sped off. Several minutes later he returned with the people in the boat and the half-submerged canoe trailing behind it. We thank the Lord that Ron was in a position to see and get help for the people.

Sometimes God uses the simple
One thing I notice about the stories of Elijah and Elisha is how often they—with God's provision—used whatever was close at hand in their ministries. For Elijah, God used flour and oil to keep him, a widow, and her son alive during a famine. Later, God used him to raise the widow's son from the dead (1 Kings 17:8–24). Another time, Elisha threw salt into a spring and the water became safe to drink again (2 Kings 2:19–22). Once, he threw flour into a stew and it removed the poison from the wild gourds (2 Kings 4:38–41). During a famine God used a gift of barley and grain given to Elisha to feed a hundred men (2 Kings 4:42–44). Likewise, in 2 Kings 6:1–7 he took a stick and threw it into the water to recover an iron ax-head. Verse 1 begins with the project they started, "The company of the prophets said to Elisha, 'Look, the place where we meet with you is too small for us.' " Apparently, Elisha would teach at the school of the prophets from time to time and their meeting place became too small. It was good news that more men wanted to join the work for God, and the students were eager to build a bigger building.

Prayer Still Moves Mountains

> "Let us go to the Jordan, where each of us can get a pole; and let us build a place there for us to meet."
>
> And he said, "Go."
>
> Then one of them said, "Won't you please come with your servants?"
>
> "I will," Elisha replied. And he went with them (2 Kings 6:2–4).

I appreciate that their leader went with them to mingle and help them. He felt comfortable being around powerful rulers as well as humble workers. Continuing on,

> They went to the Jordan and began to cut down trees. As one of them was cutting down a tree, the iron axhead fell into the water. "Oh no, my lord!" he cried out. "It was borrowed!"
>
> The man of God asked, "Where did it fall?" When he showed him the place, Elisha cut a stick and threw it there, and made the iron float. "Lift it out," he said. Then the man reached out his hand and took it (verses 4–7).

The student spontaneously cried out at his loss, and God in heaven heard his cry and impressed Elisha with a plan to meet the need. The man who had borrowed the ax may have been poor because he couldn't afford his own ax, therefore it was important to find it.

This biblical story is so short that we can easily pass over some deeper parallels. Jesus fed more than five thousand people with bread and fish, Jesus healed lepers, and Jesus raised people from the dead. Jesus multiplied fish during a fishing expedition, stilled a storm, and commanded demons to leave people. Wherever He reached out to someone with a need or someone reached out to Him, blessings followed. Most important, God raised Jesus from the dead so that we could be cleansed from sin and live with Him eternally. The ax-head that floated is just one of many stories that point to ways Jesus helped in the past and continues to point to Him as the answer to our every

So Many Ways God Helps Us

need. And He can use the simple to point to the profound.

Sometimes God bursts through strongholds
It never ceases to amaze me how God "moves mountains" standing between us and accomplishing a mission for Him. And if we note events in journals, we can see how He gets started sometimes even years in advance. It was May 1, 2011, and almost six months since being downsized from a job. I was suddenly compelled to do something commemorative on the six-month anniversary happening in ten days. First, I decided to do a modified fast for eleven days, and then, on May 11, set aside time to pray for a new beginning.

Earlier in history, God told Moses He would make the enemy nations afraid of Israel. By today's standards, Israel's army was not intimidating, but Israel had God on its side. Moses no longer had to worry about their enemies because they were worried about Israel. God often goes before us in our daily battles, preparing the way and overcoming barriers. We don't need to be worried, because God goes before us. He is on our side. He can burst through strongholds when needed.

On May 11, 2011, I drove to the Somerset Retirement complex to walk and pray along the sidewalk, and then I walked down toward the Gladstone Park Seventh-day Adventist Church. I remain in awe how God orchestrated all the loose ends going forward. He kept me busy helping people and with various projects over the next seven years. Then on April 25, 2018, I was sitting in my writing room at home when I lifted some paperwork and found some old resumes of mine. Through the years, I had applied for a few jobs even though I had a part-time job at Mourning Glory Ministries with Georgia Shaffer. I needed another part time job. That day, suddenly, I felt discouraged that none of those resumes had netted anything. So I took them upstairs, put them in the shredder, and said to myself, "This isn't working. Someone will just have to ask me!" A few hours later I met Corleen at three o'clock at a Thai food restaurant. She had wanted to take me out for a belated birthday lunch. We had a nice time chatting, but part way through,

Prayer Still Moves Mountains

she asked, "Did you know that the Gladstone Park Church is looking for someone to work in their office? You should apply." I asked a few questions about it and knew I needed to pray about it.

I soon had an interview with three people from the Gladstone Park Church. Then on May 11, 2018—which was precisely seven years after I had prayed a prayer for a new beginning—Pastor Nate told me that I got the job at the Gladstone Park Church. This is a great example of ways God helps us.

I have been very blessed to work with people who also believe God can do big things through prayer and a willingness to move forward in faith. I love the way the church makes ministry events happen like Follow the Star, Follow the Lamb, and other community outreach events. And I am encouraged that though there may be obstacles in the way, God can burst through any stronghold He wants to for ministries for His kingdom. We should never forget this.

God always forgives us

Have you ever had someone eat your last cupcake? My mom made me gluten-free carrot cake muffins for my birthday a few times, and one year, Ron ate the last one. Or maybe someone ate your last Kudo bar. I remember while on a mission trip in the Philippines, Corleen had brought a box of Kudo bars. A few days into our time there, I noticed her eating one. She said to me, "Feel free to help yourself to some Kudo bars." Apparently, this invitation only applied up until the last bar. A few days later, she was surprised to discover that I had taken the last one. When we apologize to someone—"I am so sorry that I ate your last cupcake [or Kudo bar]"—they seem to readily forgive us. And we believe them. They shrug it off, saying, "That's OK. I forgive you."

However, when Adam and Eve ate from the tree that God said not to eat from and He asked them about it, they immediately got defensive. They didn't apologize. Man blamed the woman. Woman blamed the serpent. God turned to the serpent and cursed it, and then gave a promise of hope, "And I will put enmity between you and the woman, and between your offspring and hers; he will crush your head, and you

So Many Ways God Helps Us

will strike his heel" (Genesis 3:15). This verse is a reference to Jesus Christ, the Son of God. Satan would try to destroy Christ, but Jesus would have the ultimate victory on our behalf. All who are in Christ will celebrate the victory with Him for eternity.

What if we are talking about more than cupcakes or Kudos bars? What if we accidentally killed someone? Would we be forgiven? By others? Or most important, by God? Would God forgive us, and could we still be in the kingdom for eternity? We know that King David killed Uriah on purpose because he wanted to hide his sin of sleeping with Bathsheba, Uriah's wife. David reflects on forgiveness in Psalm 32 and Psalm 51. Let's look at Psalm 32:1, 2, "Blessed is the one whose transgressions are forgiven, whose sins are covered. Blessed is the one whose sin the Lord does not count against them and in whose spirit is no deceit." Right there David says he is blessed because his sins are forgiven. Even so, many people still debate whether God forgives us. In a deeper look through the eyes of a Bible commentary, it says, "Many Christians . . . strive to keep their sins 'confessed up to date,' a noble objective, but one that has merit only if the confession has in each case been accompanied by an expulsion of sin."[1] Continuing on, "This was the experience of David and he grasped it by faith. It was on this basis that he obtained forgiveness for his sin. His repentance was genuine. He loathed the sin of which he had been guilty."[2] Then the commentary highlights the words "imputeth not." Those words are used in the New King James Version, "Blessed is the man to whom the Lord does not impute iniquity." The commentary shares, "That is, God does not reckon the sin to the sinners account. God not only forgives sin but also accepts the truly repentant as if he had never sinned."[3]

The apostle Paul repeats David's words of Psalm 32:1, 2 in Romans 4. First, he profiles Abraham, saying, "Abraham believed God, and it was credited to him as righteousness" (Romans 4:3). A little later he credits those with faith as righteous then refers to David's verses. Later, in verse 23, 24, Paul encourages readers, "The words 'it was credited to him' were written not for him alone, but also for us, to whom God

Prayer Still Moves Mountains

will credit righteousness—for us who believe in him who raised Jesus our Lord from the dead." That's a praise!

Jesus paid our debt once and for all:

> "This is the covenant I will make with them
>   after that time, says the Lord.
> I will put my laws in their hearts,
>   and I will write them on their minds."

Then [the Holy Spirit] adds:

> "Their sins and lawless acts
>   I will remember no more."

And where these have been forgiven, sacrifice for sin is no longer necessary (Hebrews 10:16–18).

We are not still sacrificing lambs or wringing our hands thinking our sins are not forgiven, because our Friend, Jesus Christ, has said they are forgiven.

Let us always remember:

- We believe God created the world.
- We believe He has always had a plan to save us.
- We believe He died in our place.
- We believe He who is in us "is greater than the one who is in the world" (1 John 4:1).
- We believe He will give us all we "need from day to day if [we] will make the Kingdom of God [our] primary concern" (Luke 12:31, TLB).
- We believe we should search the Scriptures so we can give a reason for our faith.
- We believe in the Resurrection.
- We believe He's coming back again.

So Many Ways God Helps Us

- We believe we will be with Him forever.

Wait, do we really believe He has forgiven us? How does that change how we live our lives now?

What forgiveness means to me
When I was seven weeks old, there was a court hearing to determine whether I could live with my new family or if I had to stay in the court system. Prayer and God won out, and I forever have a picture of what the "great controversy" personally looks like. It's a battle over our very lives. God gave me a family that would be perfect to raise me up with godly values, personal devotions, Christian schools, and the knowledge of not only a church family but also a worldwide church family. There is nothing better than this, except for what is soon to come—forever with Jesus! At every opportunity, I love to share with people that Jesus is coming soon. I am forever grateful to witness every time someone approaches Him for forgiveness or a relationship and He races over to be close.

God's forgiveness means that I love talking with Jesus *now*. I love talking about my day, discussing what we will do together, asking for His help to be in the right place at the right time to bless others, and helping others understand that He loves them too.

It feels as though we chat often, lifting up a prayer for any and all things—even about standing on a table to put up a picture. One day, shortly after I began working at Gladstone Park Church, I carried in a large picture to hang on the wall. Even though it seemed simple, I prayed, "Lord, I need You to help me with this. I can't hold the other end of the picture and the table looks a little wobbly." I climbed up onto the table and measured where two nails should go in the wall and put the picture on them. As I started to turn around, the table wobbled slightly and I started to fall backward. I felt myself lose my balance and in a split second thought, *Oh no!* The next second I felt a presence lift me back up and at the same time turn me around so that I faced forward instead of backward. Then I jumped down and praised

Prayer Still Moves Mountains

the Lord for my angel that intervened and kept me from falling off. I said, "Lord, thank You so much for my angel helper. I would have hurt myself, and I am so thankful for Your protection."

It is best to focus on our friend Jesus moment-by-moment, day-by-day. He forgives me when I ask. First John 1:9 shares, "If we confess our sins, he is faithful and just and will forgive us our sins and purify us from all unrighteousness." Always God wants to be with us and forgive us.

The payoff

Some people like to jump to the end of the story to see how it ends. It is encouraging to do this. Galatians 3:26 shares, "So in Christ Jesus you are all children of God through faith." It continues, that if we are Christ's, then we are also Abraham's seed and heirs of the promise. It is what Jesus has been promising all along—eternal life. Yes! Now let's jump to the end of the book to see what we will receive.

> And I heard a loud voice from the throne saying, "Look! God's dwelling place is now among the people, and he will dwell with them. They will be his people, and God himself will be with them and be their God. 'He will wipe every tear from their eyes. There will be no more death' or mourning or crying or pain, for the old order of things has passed away." He who was seated on the throne said, "I am making everything new!" Then he said, "Write this down, for these words are trustworthy and true. He said to me: 'It is done. I am the Alpha and the Omega, the Beginning and the End. To the thirsty I will give water without cost from the spring of the water of life. Those who are victorious will inherit all this, and I will be their God and they will be my children' " (Revelation 21:3–7).

How's that for the awesome promise that God has made to us—eternal life. There are so many ways God helps us. And in turn, we

So Many Ways God Helps Us

wait on God, we pray that God will help others through us, and we seek a closer walk with God.

Reflection

1. Noah found favor with God. We, too, find favor with Him. How has the covenant God made with those in the Bible blessed you as well?

2. Journal, or share with someone, about a time when God helped you help another person.

3. Has God broken down a "stronghold" for you? Please journal the story so you don't forget it. If you have another "stronghold" to overcome, consider inquiring what God wants you to do.

4. What are you sharing with others about your future home in heaven?

---

1. Francis D. Nichol, *The Seventh-day Adventist Bible Commentary*, vol. 3, rev. ed. (Washington DC: Review and Herald®, 1980), 706.
2. Nichol, 706.
3. Nichol, 706.

Chapter 8

With Us in the Wait

The eyes of the LORD *are on the righteous,*
and his ears are attentive to their cry.

—Psalm 34:15

I couldn't reach you on your cell phone? Did you have it off? I called because I don't feel right. It feels like my headed exploded inside," my mother shared when she finally reached me.

"Oh no! All right, I'm on my way to you," I replied. I hung up and jumped into my truck. As I called a friend for prayer, I thought, *We probably need to go to the ER and make sure it's not a stroke.*

Upon arrival, my mother was lying on her bed looking pink and flushed. She slowly sat up, grabbed her purse, and we headed to the ER. The fact that she could move made me think it probably wasn't a stroke, but what had happened? We checked in at a temporary desk in the middle of the waiting room. As I began to glance around, my heart sank as the reality set in that there were more than thirty people also waiting. *Oh my, all these people are waiting for the twenty-five emergency beds they have?* We had a seat and to my astonishment a doctor soon stepped from around a temporary curtain and asked my mother questions. Then they put her on a bed behind another temporary curtain for an EKG test. *This is like an army field hospital situation or a disaster site where they don't have any room in the regular ER,* I thought.

Have you ever waited for something? My parents waited four years to have me. I've been waiting decades for Jesus to come. In Joshua 1:5,

With Us in the Wait

God said to Joshua, who was Moses' assistant, "As I was with Moses, so I will be with you." I am so thankful that God promises to be with us while we wait. Then God encouraged Joshua in Joshua 1:8, "Keep this Book of the Law always on your lips; meditate on it day and night, so that you may be careful to do everything written in it. Then you will be prosperous and successful." In order to follow this counsel, we must hold on to God's hand no matter what. He will walk with us through every challenge we face.

After Mom's EKG, we sat down to wait for room in the blood-testing area. I looked around and began to notice the other people who were also waiting. One woman moaned and cried loudly to the friend seated beside her, "I need to get in there. I'm not going to make it. I'm going to faint. Why is it going so slow? I'm not going to make it! I'm not going to make it!" She was bent over with a bag, just in case she threw up. I started praying silently.

A man in a wheelchair five feet away from us did throw up. I said to my mother, "It doesn't bother me, but if it bothers you we can move." Instantly she was on her feet and moved to a chair five feet away but out of the line of vision.

"Our child has a temperature of 104, and they gave us some medicine but we need to get in there," a father said about his wife clutching a crying baby that caught my attention. The room was cold because the outside door kept opening. I gave my coat to my mother. No one was handing out water or Kleenex or snacks or praying with these people. *What a need someone could fill. What's the backstory to all these people?* I wondered.

Hearing the pleas of the people around us pulled me right in, and I longed to throw my arms around the crying ones, hear more details, and pray with hope to the One who truly can heal. I love the assurance of Psalm 34:15, "The eyes of the Lord are on the righteous, and his ears are attentive to their cry." Let's not ignore anyone God puts in front of us—if nothing else, we can lift a silent prayer on their behalf. The next thing I heard in the hospital was, "I hit him hard and broke my hand. But I want you to be looking for a Chevy truck that I chased away."

Prayer Still Moves Mountains

A man who held his hand on an ice pack was speaking to someone on his phone.

Time seemed to stand still. All we could do was wait, and wait, and wait—for an opening in the main room, where they had twenty-five beds for lucky people who were lying back getting medical help. *What did I do?* I wondered. *If my mother turns out fine, then I wasted her evening and her money. She doesn't look like she had a stroke. If I could turn back the clock, would I then change the choice that brought us here, or are my silent prayers making a difference here?*

Special door of opportunity

As we waited at the ER, every so often the "special door" would open and a nurse would stand there and call a name and the waiting-room patient would walk toward the door for help. Each time the door opened we all turned our heads in hope that it was our turn to be called. We all wanted the same thing—hope and help.

John 5 shares about a similar "door" of opportunity—a place where sick people waited by a pool for the stirring of the water and, it was said, whoever stepped in first was cured. When I think about this story, I imagine a chaotic scene with many people trying to reach help. Yet, our heavenly Father can still make "God moments" happen in the chaos. Let's read it.

> Some time later, Jesus went up to Jerusalem for one of the Jewish festivals. Now there is in Jerusalem near the Sheep Gate a pool, which in Aramaic is called Bethesda and which is surrounded by five covered colonnades. Here a great number of disabled people used to lie—the blind, the lame, the paralyzed—and they waited for the moving of the waters. From time to time an angel of the Lord would come down and stir up the waters. The first one into the pool after each such disturbance would be cured of whatever disease they had. One who was there had been an invalid for thirty-eight years.

With Us in the Wait

I waited sixteen years to graduate from college but thinking about waiting for thirty-eight years for help—wow! We might wait for something for a long time, but knowing that God is working on putting the pieces of our lives together in preparation for His coming encourages us.

Let's continue reading.

> When Jesus saw him lying there and learned that he had been in this condition for a long time, he asked him, "Do you want to get well?"
>
> "Sir," the invalid replied, "I have no one to help me into the pool when the water is stirred. While I am trying to get in, someone else goes down ahead of me."
>
> Then Jesus said to him, "Get up! Pick up your mat and walk." At once the man was cured; he picked up his mat and walked.
>
> The day on which this took place was a Sabbath, and so the Jewish leaders said to the man who had been healed, "It is the Sabbath; the law forbids you to carry your mat."
>
> But he replied, "The man who made me well said to me, 'Pick up your mat and walk.' "
>
> So they asked him, "Who is this fellow who told you to pick it up and walk?" (John 5:6–12).

It is interesting that they asked, "Who?" I think the religious leaders knew the "who." They just wanted confirmation as evidence against Jesus. Verses 13 and 14 share, "The man who was healed had no idea who it was, for Jesus had slipped away into the crowd that was there. Later Jesus found him at the temple and said to him, 'See, you are well again. Stop sinning or something worse may happen to you.' " How wonderful that Jesus reached out to this man again.

No condemnation for those who are in Christ Jesus

What did Jesus mean when He told the man to "sin no more" (NKJV)?

Prayer Still Moves Mountains

Everyone is a sinner, so how can we overcome sin? First off, we have to know what sin is. Romans 7:7 says, "What shall we say, then? Is the law sinful? Certainly not! Nevertheless, I would not have known what sin was had it not been for the law. For I would not have known what coveting really was if the law had not said, 'You shall not covet.' " Later on, Paul laments, "We know that the law is spiritual; but I am unspiritual, sold as a slave to sin. I do not understand what I do. For what I want to do I do not do, but what I hate I do" (Romans 7:14, 15). Thus even Paul couldn't stop sinning by his own effort. However, Paul joyfully exclaims, "Therefore, there is now no condemnation for those who are in Christ Jesus" (Romans 8:1). This is the joy Jesus wanted the man healed from thirty-eight years of suffering to experience. He wanted him to be controlled by the Spirit of God.

Sometimes waiting is good

Mom's turn finally came, and we were ushered through the special door into the ER. After four hours of waiting, Mom felt better and as the doctor reviewed the tests that had been taken it was decided that there was nothing wrong. Looking back, I think she had a reaction to some food, and it just took some time for her to feel better.

The Bible calls us to look after one another. Philippians 2:4 shares, "Not looking to your own interests but each of you to the interests of the others." Jesus always looked after others. Here are some biblical examples of Jesus personally reaching out to others. And these people saw incredible things happen *because* they waited.

To the disciples in the boat, Matthew 14:27 shares, "But Jesus immediately said to them: 'Take courage! It is I. Don't be afraid.' " As Jesus continued to walk across the water, Peter stepped out of the boat and walked on the water; however, when he saw the wind he was afraid and beginning to sink, cried out for help. I love Jesus' response as His hand reaches out to Peter, "Immediately Jesus reached out his hand and caught him. 'You of little faith,' he said, 'why did you doubt?' " (verse 31).

To the man with leprosy in Matthew 8:2, 3,

With Us in the Wait

> A man with leprosy came and knelt before him and said, "Lord, if you are willing, you can make me clean."
> Jesus reached out his hand and touched the man. "I am willing," he said. "Be clean!" Immediately he was cleansed of his leprosy."

To the blind in Matthew 9:27–30,

> As Jesus went on from there, two blind men followed him, calling out, "Have mercy on us, Son of David!"
> When he had gone indoors, the blind men came to him, and he asked them, "Do you believe that I am able to do this?"
> "Yes, Lord," they replied.
> Then he touched their eyes and said, "According to your faith let it be done to you"; and their sight was restored.

In response to the four thousand people who were hungry, He broke bread with His hands in Matthew 15:36–38, "Then he took the seven loaves and the fish, and when he had given thanks, he broke them and gave them to the disciples, and they in turn to the people. They all ate and were satisfied. Afterward the disciples picked up seven basketfuls of broken pieces that were left over. The number of those who ate was four thousand men, besides women and children."

To the paralytic in Matthew 9:1, 2, "Jesus stepped into a boat, crossed over and came to his own town. Some men brought to him a paralyzed man, lying on a mat. When Jesus saw their faith, he said to the man, 'Take heart, son; your sins are forgiven.' " And verses 6–8 share that Jesus touches *and* forgives sin, "But I want you to know that the Son of Man has authority on earth to forgive sins.' So he said to the paralyzed man, 'Get up, take your mat and go home.' Then the man got up and went home. When the crowd saw this, they were filled with awe; and they praised God, who had given such authority to man."

In these stories, Jesus gave courage, touched and healed the sick, fed

Prayer Still Moves Mountains

the hungry, and forgave sins. Jesus longs to reach out and touch us, too, while we are waiting for His return.

Touched by an angel

For about nine years after my father was diagnosed with Alzheimer's, my mom watched him slowly decline. It was like losing someone piece by agonizing piece. Even so, she selflessly cared for him. She had help from Mark, a caretaker, and I helped whenever possible, but it was still wearying work. She couldn't turn her back for a minute because my dad was constantly moving and getting into things. She often fell asleep at the table. Thankfully, she's better rested now, though we miss my dad greatly.

On March 21, 2021, a Sunday, I was praying for people and thinking about how I believe that God can do anything, and I believe He loves to be close and to comfort His people. When I got to my mom's name, I said, "Please keep doing special things for my mother. Would You touch her with the angel or something to let her know You're with her?" I reached out my hand as if in emphasis. Then I went about my tasks. Later in the day, I called Mom to ask how her day was going.

She said, "Probably the biggest thing that happened was that I fell asleep at the table after lunch and then I felt a *tap, tap, tap, tap* on my shoulder. My angel tapped me on my shoulder and woke me up."

It took a moment for the reality to sink in as I listened. She lives alone. I paused, then asked, "Your angel tapped you on your shoulder?"

"Yes, my angel really tapped me," she replied.

What a surprising answer to my morning prayer! I immediately thought of the story of Mary on Resurrection day. It's recorded in John 20:1, 2, "Early on the first day of the week, while it was still dark, Mary Magdalene went to the tomb and saw that the stone had been removed from the entrance. So she came running to Simon Peter and the other disciple, the one Jesus loved, and said, 'They have taken the Lord out of the tomb, and we don't know where they have put him!' "

Picture Peter and John running to the tomb—Peter enters the tomb first followed by John. The strips of linen were in place, but Jesus wasn't

With Us in the Wait

there. It says John saw and believed. Then they went back to where they were staying. However, Mary didn't go back with them. I find that interesting. She stayed as if in shock at all that had happened—when something dramatic happens to those we love, it can take a while to sink in. I think the times we need comfort the most is when God does big things and reaches in to remind us of His love. And when we feel empathy for another person, He does something special. As women, we have a nurturing mentoring instinct built into us. Like when I had a moment of prayerful empathy for my mother. "Please keep doing special things for my mother. Would You touch her with the angel or something to let her know You're with her?"

John continues,

> Now Mary stood outside the tomb crying. As she wept, she bent over to look into the tomb and saw two angels in white, seated where Jesus' body had been, one at the head and the other at the foot.
>
> They asked her, "Woman, why are you crying?"
>
> "They have taken my Lord away," she said, "and I don't know where they have put him." At this, she turned around and saw Jesus standing there, but she did not realize that it was Jesus.
>
> He asked her, "Woman, why are you crying? Who is it you are looking for?"
>
> Thinking he was the gardener, she said, "Sir, if you have carried him away, tell me where you have put him, and I will get him."
>
> Jesus said to her, "Mary" (John 20:11–16).

Jesus wanted to comfort her! I love that personal "touch" by Jesus reaching out to His hurting friend. And He still comforts us today.

Rejoining my conversation with my mother, I said, "This must make you feel very special."

She replied, "Yes it does."

Prayer Still Moves Mountains

After a bit I hung up the phone, and I marveled thinking about the unseen angel reaching in and touching my mom just because I asked. So I lifted a thank You prayer. What an incredibly reassuring picture of God reaching out to us right now as we wait for His soon return. There are so many ways God is with us in the wait!

Reflection

1. How do you deal with waiting in a doctor's office or emergency room?

2. Read the whole story of Mary in John 20 as she is distraught because her Friend died. Share with someone or journal how it would make you feel to be comforted by Jesus.

3. How does it feel to be forgiven by Jesus for your sin? If you are not sure, please reach out to a pastor, elder, or friend to share how you are feeling instead.

Chapter 9

Just How Much Anger Is Enough?

Get rid of all bitterness, rage and anger, brawling and slander, along with every form of malice.
—Ephesians 4:31

"Just how much anger is enough?" my friend Georgia Shaffer, the Pennsylvania psychologist I work for, asked me one day after I shared about a friend erupting in anger at me yet again.

"When she gets angry, she can yell for a long time—this time it lasted about twenty minutes. A previous time, her angry yelling lasted for over an hour. Since I was a passenger in the car, I felt as if I was being held captive. It was awful! It feels like the devil is yelling at me through her. She's told me that she just gives in to her anger because it is easier than fighting it," I replied.

"Maybe you should step away from that friendship. It's unhealthy to listen to anger directed at us again and again. It is harmful to our brains and our health," Georgia replied.

"You are so right. I often feel confused and hurt after our encounters. Later she doesn't remember what she said, so it's difficult, if not impossible, to find a resolution," I replied.

In his letter to the believers in Ephesus, Paul counseled them to avoid anger. Ephesians 4:30–32 shares, "And do not grieve the Holy Spirit of God, with whom you were sealed for the day of redemption. Get rid of all bitterness, rage and anger, brawling and slander, along with every form of malice. Be kind and compassionate to one another,

Prayer Still Moves Mountains

forgiving each other, just as in Christ God forgave you."

Georgia's question to me that day is a good one—just how much anger is enough? In Zechariah 3 we read that the devil stood beside Joshua to accuse him. Our accuser the devil never gives up his anger against us. Revelation 12:10 describes the devil as the one "who accuses them before our God day and night." For some people, anger is a stronghold that they cling to; others may not have experienced God's grace for themselves so they don't know how to extend it to others.

What to do when your anger is out of control
Early in 2021, Georgia Shaffer wrote an article titled *How to Reduce Your Anger*, and she said I could share her four points here. She recommends "a few strategies that may help you reduce your anger when those feelings come roaring to the surface."[1]

Hit Pause
Before you let loose with a barrage of angry words, hit an imaginary pause button, take several deep breaths, and count to 10. Taking a moment to stop, pray and think enables us to consider our response rather than immediately lashing out.

Monitor Your Thoughts
Pay attention to what you say to yourself because some thoughts are anger-provoking. Ask, "What am I thinking that makes me feel this way?" If you realize you are repeating something to yourself that ignites your rage, reframe the thought into something positive to help douse your fury.

Remember Successful Strategies
When tension rises, think about times when you were angry but didn't explode or do something regrettable. If you're having trouble thinking of a time when you maintained your cool, here are some ideas to help you blow off steam safely: run around the block, lift weights, beat a pillow, hoe the

Just How Much Anger Is Enough?

garden, mow the grass, or whatever positive activity gets your heart pumping and shifts your thoughts.

Identify Who or What Drives You Crazy
No matter how great a day you're having or how good your mood is, there may be one person or situation that can quickly sour your disposition. Being aware of our triggers can put us on the path to reacting differently to them. Whether we learn to accept things as they are or change our responses to them, we are taking the responsibility to minimize the intensity of our anger and lessen any subsequent fallout.[2]

Maintaining peace in the journey

Do you want peace in your life? I remember a time in my life when God pointed out an issue that kept causing anxious thoughts to fill my mind. It occurred a few days before April 28, 2015, when Corleen and I planned to drive to eastern Oregon and tour the Ronald McDonald house and ask how my local church could help the organization. On the way, I shared with Corleen how God had pointed out something I was holding on to and that I wanted to create a memory for letting it go. Then whenever I thought about it again, I would remember my action and say, "No, I let that go."

"Do you mind if we go by Drake Park in Bend and have a 'let go prayer'?" I asked. I want to write something on a rock and then throw it into the river."

"That's a unique idea. I might try that too," she responded. We drove to Drake Park and walked toward a picnic table by the water. My Bible was in my hand, and I was ready to look up a verse when Corleen said, "Hey, you could use 'cast your cares on the Lord and he will sustain you.' I don't know where it is found though."

I replied, "Good one, that is Psalm 55:22, and there's more, 'he will never let the righteous be shaken.' " I opened the Bible to that promise, claimed it, and then said a prayer. Corleen found two stones, and we said a prayer for something she wanted to lay down and then

Prayer Still Moves Mountains

we walked over to the bridge and threw in our rocks. It felt good to let an issue go. And Jesus promises us peace. Psalm 29:11 says, "The LORD gives strength to his people; the LORD blesses his people with peace."

Jonah had more anger than peace

In the story of Jonah, we often see pride and anger through his words and actions. God called Jonah to deliver a message of judgment to the people of Nineveh, but he didn't want to go. Jonah lived in the golden age of the Northern Kingdom. Under Jeroboam II, Jonah had a role in the recovery of a weakened Israel. Second Kings 14:25 reflects that Jeroboam was influenced by Jonah, "He was the one who restored the boundaries of Israel from Lebo Hamath to the Dead Sea, in accordance with the word of the LORD, the God of Israel, spoken through his servant Jonah son of Amittai, the prophet from Gath Hepher." Jonah likely enjoyed the favor of both Jeroboam II and his fellow citizens.

No wonder the divine command to go to Nineveh—the capital of the Assyrian nation that attacked the people of Israel many times—came as a jolting shock. The Bible indicates that Jonah reacted immediately to the divine commission, "But Jonah ran away from the LORD and headed for Tarshish" (Jonah 1:3). It was easy to be God's spokesman when the message was positive, but in the face of delivering a message of judgment to the enemy, Jonah's anger and unwillingness asserted itself. Jonah's assignment was to deliver the "Let sin go" message—to say something like, "Turn from sin or you will be destroyed"—and he highly doubted his message would be popular or that it would achieve results.

Continuing on with the story, we read, "He went down to Joppa, where he found a ship bound for that port. After paying the fare, he went aboard and sailed for Tarshish to flee from the LORD" (verse 3). It looked as if he was safe for a time, but "then the LORD sent a great wind on the sea, and such a violent storm arose that the ship threatened to break up. All the sailors were afraid and each cried out to his own god. And they threw the cargo into the sea to lighten the ship. But Jonah had gone below deck, where he lay down and fell into a deep sleep" (1:4).

Sin may rock you to sleep, but it is not a restful sleep. Matthew

Just How Much Anger Is Enough?

Henry observed, "Sin brings storms and tempests into the soul, into the family, into churches and nations; it is a disquieting, disturbing thing."[3] You may forget sin is there. You may forget you were ever holding on to it. Others may forget you were ever holding on to it. But God remembers. If we pray to be changed, He will lead us to repentance. In Jonah's case, God wanted to point it out because the fate of a whole nation was at stake.

Do you want peace in your life or do you want to hold on to difficulties? Philippians 3:12 urges, "Not that I have already obtained all this, or have already arrived at my goal, but I press on to take hold of that for which Christ Jesus took hold of me. Brothers and sisters, I do not count myself yet to have taken hold of it. But one thing I do: Forgetting what is behind and straining toward what is ahead." Like Paul, I urge you to let go and accept the peace God freely offers instead.

Are you holding on to something you shouldn't? Unclench your fist, go running to God, and leave it in His more-than-capable hands.

Undealt-with issues can cause storms

Jonah 1:6–7 reveals that

> the captain went to [Jonah] and said, "How can you sleep? Get up and call on your god! Maybe he will take notice of us so that we will not perish."
>
> Then the sailors said to each other, "Come, let us cast lots to find out who is responsible for this calamity." They cast lots and the lot fell on Jonah.

It is interesting that he had to encounter a storm before he was willing to admit fault. This resulted in his urging them, " 'Pick me up and throw me into the sea,' he replied, 'and it will become calm. I know that it is my fault that this great storm has come upon you' " (verse 12).

So Jonah took three steps: first, he admitted fault; second, he took steps to erase the problem or issue (talk to someone, destroy the item, etc.); and third, he ran to God and rededicated himself to Him. Then

Prayer Still Moves Mountains

Jonah did what he thought was the only way to save the others and said, "Throw me overboard." They did, and the sea calmed. It seems that Jonah would drown and that would be the end of the story; however, our God isn't like that. At least when it comes to pardon—God always forgives when we ask (see 1 John 1:9). As he thought about how God had dealt with him, Jonah offered this prayer, "But I, with shouts of grateful praise, will sacrifice to you. What I have vowed I will make good. I will say, 'Salvation comes from the Lord' " (Jonah 2:9).

Then "the Lord commanded the fish, and it vomited Jonah onto dry land" (verse 10). I find it encouraging that God continues using us for His service even while He points out sins that have become idols. "Then the word of the Lord came to Jonah a second time, 'Go to the great city of Nineveh and proclaim to it the message I give you.' Jonah obeyed the word of the Lord and went to Nineveh" (Jonah 3:1–3). Essentially, he said, *It's my fault. I am throwing the issue overboard. I want peace.* Now he's not afraid of the gospel.

Jonah shared a short message, in essence, "Repent or die." The Ninevites believed God, and they followed the three steps to repentance:

- Step one—admit fault, "Let them give up their evil ways and their violence" (Jonah 3:8).
- Step two—take steps to erase the problem, "The Ninevites believed God. A fast was proclaimed, and all of them, from the greatest to the least, put on sackcloth" (verse 5).
- Step three—run to Jesus and rededicate yourself to Him. Jonah 3:8 shares that they said, "Let everyone call urgently on God."

It is wonderful how God instantly responded with forgiveness: "When God saw what they did and how they turned from their evil ways, he relented and did not bring on them the destruction he had threatened" (verse 10). Our great and compassionate God is like that. But once again, Jonah got angry. Jonah 4:1, shares, "But to Jonah this seemed very wrong, and he became angry." Anger stands in the way of God's wholistic purpose for us. And anger is not only a sin but also a doorway to other sins.

Just How Much Anger Is Enough?

The anger-as-a-temptation-to-further-sin idea became clear to me while observing at a men's conference years ago while I was working in Women's Ministries (at that time it also included Men's Ministries). Sabbath morning at the conference eight men sat on a panel to discuss pornography. The consensus on the panel seemed to be, *Yes, it's an issue, but we must hold on to Christ in the battle and trust that He will help us overcome.*

Then Pastor George stood up to share a short message. He shared Romans 7:15, "For what I want to do I do not do, but what I hate I do." Then he reminded us that Romans 8:1 assures us, "Therefore, there is now no condemnation for those who are in Christ Jesus." And verse 5 and 6 shares, "Those who live according to the flesh have their minds set on what the flesh desires; but those who live in accordance with the Spirit have their minds set on what the Spirit desires. The mind governed by the flesh is death, but the mind governed by the Spirit is life and peace."

Pastor George also mentioned that there are four trigger points that pave the way to giving into temptation, and these are represented by the acronym HALT. He said, "When you are Hungry, Angry, Lonely, or Tired, you are vulnerable. In any of these situations it is best to HALT and run to Jesus." What a simple practice to help us escape temptation!

Jonah wouldn't let go

For a second time Jonah was very angry, and

> he prayed to the LORD, "Isn't this what I said, LORD, when I was still at home? That is what I tried to forestall by fleeing to Tarshish. I knew that you are a gracious and compassionate God, slow to anger and abounding in love, a God who relents from sending calamity. Now, LORD, take away my life, for it is better for me to die than to live."
>
> But the LORD replied, "Is it right for you to be angry?" (Jonah 4:2–4).

Prayer Still Moves Mountains

Despite Jonah's new fit of anger, God was gracious and compassionate and longed to hear him again say the words he said earlier, "It is my fault." He wanted him to add: "Take the anger that I am holding onto. I need You, Lord, help me to let this anger go." Instead, Jonah held on to his anger. So God sent him a loving illustration through a vine, some shade, and finally, a worm that ate the vine. Even so, Jonah remained angry.

> But God said to Jonah, "Is it right for you to be angry about the plant?"
> "It is," he said. "And I'm so angry I wish I were dead."
> But the LORD said, "You have been concerned about this plant, though you did not tend it or make it grow. It sprang up overnight and died overnight. And should I not have concern for the great city of Nineveh, in which there are more than a hundred and twenty thousand people who cannot tell their right hand from their left—and also many animals?" (verses 9, 10).

Jonah left this question unanswered, and the Bible doesn't record the rest of Jonah's story elsewhere. One lesson we can learn from Jonah's life is how easily anger can lead us straight into temptation.

How much anger is enough

I've learned that there are "proactive" people and "reactive" people. "Proactive" people have a nurturing, healing, and encouraging effect on you. "Reactive" people have a negative, poisonous effect on you. Toxic, angry people leave a trail behind them of destroyed jobs and friendships, and they try to undermine your God-given calling. As Christians, we need to know what our ministry and purpose are supposed to be, and those should take precedence over "reactive" people. In other words, like Nehemiah, be alert to anyone and anything that steals our attention and time away from the mission God has called us to.

It may help to ask ourselves these questions: Is their anger keeping us awake at night? Do they destroy our peace, strength, joy, and hope? Do we feel minimized by them? Are they trying to control us? Then consider

Just How Much Anger Is Enough?

how Jesus responded to toxic people. Jesus only let Himself be persecuted once—on the cross. Other times He walked away or let others walk away. Jesus kept focused on His mission. Gary Thomas, in his book *When to Walk Away*, shares, "The call to seek first the kingdom of God is the foundation for how we can biblically respond to toxic people."[4] In his introduction, he states, "We can't let others steal our joy or our mission. It's time to strengthen our defense, learn to set good boundaries, and focus on our God-given purpose."[5]

What about us?

If we are the one who struggles with anger issues, then consider praying, "Lord, please show me what I'm holding on to that keeps me responding in anger." If we already know the issue, then we confess it and release it into God's hands. Whenever God brings conviction to our hearts and minds, take a moment to pray, "Lord, give me boldness so that when You remind me of what I am holding on to, I will immediately give it to You. I want to proclaim the gospel to anyone You put in my path. Thank You for forgiveness and Your blood that cleanses me from all sin. In Jesus' name, amen."

Peter's story of repentance and new opportunity

The apostle Peter is a good example of someone who was brash, often spoke too quickly, and then became fearful and denied Jesus Christ. Thankfully, he recognized his error, wept bitterly, and repented. Eventually he steadfastly fulfilled his mission and purpose for Christ. After His resurrection, Jesus sought Peter out and gave him another chance:

> "Early in the morning, Jesus stood on the shore, but the disciples did not realize that it was Jesus.
> He called out to them, "Friends, haven't you any fish?"
> "No," they answered.
> He said, "Throw your net on the right side of the boat and you will find some." When they did, they were unable to haul the net in because of the large number of fish (John 21:4–6).

After meeting Jesus on the shore and enjoying a bread and fish

Prayer Still Moves Mountains

breakfast, three times Jesus asked Peter if he loved Him and then responded to Peter these three ways: "Feed my lambs," "Take care of my sheep" and "Feed my sheep" (verses 15–17).

Jesus led him through Peter's public repentance of his denial by asking the question three times. His identity changed from rash and hasty to a "rock" for Jesus.

I am thankful for a God who relents from sending calamity. A God who longs to hear us say, "Help me, I'm having trouble with this sin problem. Do whatever You need to do to take this problem away. I rededicate myself to You." And when we name it and throw it into the river, then the Lord blesses us with peace and we receive our next instructions.

Reflection

1. Reflect on Georgia's suggestions on ways to reduce your anger or another sin issue. Write out some ways that would work for you to release anger or other issues and throw them out of your life.

2. Do you have people in your life who are holding you hostage with their anger? Consider ways to distance yourself.

3. Write out your ministry and purpose. If you need help polishing what you have written, pray and read Scripture first for ideas that God may wish to point out. Then ask those closest to you what they see as your ministry strengths.

---

1. Georgia Shaffer, "How to Reduce Your Anger," *Georgia Shaffer: Coach. Author. Speaker,* January 29, 2021, https://georgiashaffer.com/uncategorized/stories/how-to-reduce-your-anger/.
2. Shaffer.
3. Matthew Henry, "Jonah 1 Bible Commentary," *Matthew Henry Bible Commentary* (complete), Christianity.com, accessed April 5, 2022, https://www.christianity.com/bible/commentary/matthew-henry-complete/jonah/1.
4. Gary Thomas, *When to Walk Away* (Grand Rapids, MI: Zondervan, 2019), 61.
5. Thomas, inside cover leaf.

Chapter 10

Where Do We Find Our Identity?

For this is what the Sovereign L<small>ORD</small> says: I myself will search for my sheep and look after them.
—Ezekiel 34:11

When I was younger, many people talked about intelligence quotient (IQ), and how high or low various individuals scored. Now emotional intelligence (EQ) is all the rage, and many theorize that EQ is more important than technical ability when it comes to interacting and connecting with others. Your IQ enables you to get into a good college, while your EQ helps you manage the emotions and stresses of life. Emotional intelligence is the ability to effectively "manage your own emotions and understand the emotions of people around you."[1] Emotional intelligence can be observed in others in five areas of their life: social skills, empathy, motivation, self-regulation, and self-awareness. Furthermore, "when we are aware of what makes us 'us,' we become more conscious of our own feelings and motives. More importantly, we manage how our emotions affect ourselves and others, and we don't allow those emotions to control us."[2]

I have a friend who struggles with anger, it always seems to bubble near the surface. One minute she likes you and the next she starts yelling at you. One November my friend got angry, started yelling, and closed the door on our friendship. This left me stunned and heartbroken. It all happened in just a few minutes.

It reminded me of something that happened in my mom's yard when

Prayer Still Moves Mountains

I spotted a snake lying on a large heather bush. It was a beautiful warm sunny day, and he was absorbing the warmth and rubbing his head on the flowers. I imagined him smelling them and thinking how wonderful his life was right then. My mom doesn't like snakes in the yard because they scare the birds, so I knew the snake should go. I grabbed him and walked him over behind the neighbor's yard where there were blackberry bushes and threw him onto the blackberry bushes. Instantly I thought, *You know, this is just like life. One minute you are sunning yourself and smelling the nice flowers, and the next minute someone grabs you and throws you into the blackberry bushes.*

We may have people in our lives that become angry at us and leave the friendship, but Jesus promises that He will never leave us or desert us. He sticks with us through all circumstances, and John 15:15 shares, "I no longer call you servants, because a servant does not know his master's business. Instead, I have called you friends, for everything that I learned from my Father I have made known to you."

Have you ever lost a friendship? It hurts. I was stunned and hurt by the loss of my friendship, but I was astonished when God was instant in His encouragement in this new place. The next day, my friend Georgia suggested I journal and pray about the loss. So with my Bible and Scripture promises book open, I wrote out several pages about my loss in order to start the healing process. Each place that I paused because there was pain or questioning, I said a prayer and found a verse or several verses of hope to write in that section. It was like God said to me, *Diane, will you trust Me with this? Like the Israelites who left Egypt and later thought that nothing could be better than Egypt. I have the whole picture in mind.* At the end of the year, I received an email sent from the angry friend I'd lost that said she was pondering the year and that "you are part good and part bad."

Huh? I thought. *I'm so glad God is not like this.* God doesn't hold our sins against us after we repent. Instead, He shares, "I, even I, am he who blots out your transgressions, for my own sake, and remembers your sins no more" (Isaiah 43:25). And in confident detail, Hebrews 10:17–22 tells us, "Their sins and lawless acts / I will remember no more."

Where Do We Find Our Identity?

And where these have been forgiven, sacrifice for sin is no longer necessary.

> Therefore, brothers and sisters, since we have confidence to enter the Most Holy Place by the blood of Jesus, by a new and living way opened for us through the curtain, that is, his body, and since we have a great priest over the house of God, let us draw near to God with a sincere heart and with the full assurance that faith brings, having our hearts sprinkled to cleanse us from a guilty conscience and having our bodies washed with pure water.

What wonderful assurance that when we confess our sins, our loving Savior forgives and forgets them!

I am found, I am Yours
Two months later, in January, my friend Karen phoned: "Twenty ladies from the church are going to a ladies night out event sponsored by The Fish Christian radio station. One lady has canceled, so we have space. Would you like to go?"

My friend Karen works full-time, and we don't see each other as often as we would like, so it sounded like a good connection time. Yet, I asked, "What does *ladies night out* mean?"

She replied, "They are having a dinner and then ladies from the radio station are speaking."

"That sounds fun. I'll go," I replied.

After a nice dinner and conversation with those at our tables, the speakers began. One speaker shared about a day when she was hurting and feeling lost. She went outside to take some quiet time, opened her Bible, and penned in her journal some thoughts that came to her about who she is "in Christ," and I wrote down what she projected on the screen. In Christ,

- I am found.

Prayer Still Moves Mountains

- I am Yours.
- I am loved.
- I'm made pure.
- I have life.
- I am healed.
- I am free.

She read from Jeremiah 29, but she emphasized, " 'Then you will call on me and come and pray to me, and I will listen to you. You will seek me and find me when you seek me with all your heart. I will be found by you,' declares the Lord" (verses 12–14). It reminded me, again, of the importance of knowing our identity "in Christ." I would encourage you to record the traits that belong to us when we're "in Christ." Here are two for example:

- In Christ, I am God's friend—John 15:15.
- In Christ, I am not rejected—Romans 8:1.

If we open to Psalm 34 and read, we notice it has some great identity statements, "this poor man called, and the Lord heard him" (verse 6); "the eyes of the Lord are on the righteous" (verse 15); and "no one who takes refuge in him will be condemned" (verse 22). Take some time to study the Bible and journal about the "in Christ" identity statements you find. I guarantee it will increase your faith, trust, and peace.

Paul's description of identity

Before accepting Jesus, Paul (or Saul, as he was known then) thought he was good enough, but then when he came to know Jesus, he realized that he wasn't good enough and that he never could be without Jesus. Paul wrote a lot of the New Testament, and his credentials were impeccable. Take a look at what Paul said about himself, "For it is we who are the circumcision, we who serve God by his Spirit, who boast in Christ Jesus, and who put no confidence in the flesh—though I

Where Do We Find Our Identity?

myself have reasons for such confidence. If someone else thinks he has reasons to put confidence in the flesh, I have more: circumcised on the eighth day, of the people of Israel, of the tribe of Benjamin, a Hebrew of Hebrews; in regard to the law, a Pharisee; as for zeal, persecuting the church; as for righteousness based on the law, faultless" (Philippians 3:4–6). So here are Paul's credentials:

Quality	Application
Circumcised on eighth day	Paul was a lifelong Jew
Israelite from the tribe of Benjamin	Paul belonged to the tribe who produced Israel's first king—Saul
A Hebrew of Hebrews	Paul's Hebrew pedigree was flawless
A Pharisee	Paul chose to separate himself from unholy things
Zealously persecuted the church	Paul was completely devoted to his cause
Righteousness based on law	Paul thought his effort to keep the law was faultless

Impressive list! But let's continue reading. When Paul began to follow Jesus, he quickly realized that his list no longer measured up. He couldn't be good enough, regardless of his "credentials." But in Jesus, Paul found his true identity, and he testified, "But whatever were gains to me I now consider loss for the sake of Christ. What is more, I consider everything a loss because of the surpassing worth of knowing Christ Jesus my Lord, for whose sake I have lost all things. I consider them garbage, that I may gain Christ and be found in him, not having a righteousness of my own that comes from the law, but that which is through faith in Christ—the righteousness that comes from God on the basis of faith" (verses 7–9).

The world will try to tell you that you must strive for yourself—that you have inner power all by yourself. But Jesus tells us that we need to repent of our sins and cling to Him, "Salvation is found is no one else,

Prayer Still Moves Mountains

for there is no other name under heaven given to mankind by which we must be saved" (Acts 4:12).

My shield is God Most High

One April day my mom and I were enjoying a walk through a botanical park. As we walked along the path, my mom saw a child I didn't see. She quickly said to me, "I just saw a kid that was wearing a shirt with a verse on it. It was Psalm 1:10." I hesitated a moment as I thought, *I don't think Psalm 1 has ten verses. I find Psalm 1 interesting because it is short and has a memorable description that shares if we walk with sinners, soon we will stop to stand with them and then we will be so like them that we sit and partake with them.*

I replied to her, "Where is the child? I don't think Psalm 1 has ten verses." She pointed, but we didn't see him. As I set out in earnest to walk in that direction and rounded a corner, I soon saw him. He was a cute little boy about five years old with light brown hair and a tan shirt that read simply, "Psalm 7:10." His shirt didn't have the mass-produced look because it was just simple wording on a shirt, and I began to wonder, *His mother must have made the shirt just for him, and if she had just one verse from the whole Bible to choose, this verse must have special meaning.* I couldn't wait to get home to see what the verse said! Later I opened my Bible to read, "My shield is God Most High, who saves the upright in heart" (Psalm 7:10). That is the identity I want too!

The Bible portrays the battle of identity

The battle of identity begins with Lucifer in heaven—he intented to be like the Most High and overthrow God's kingdom. Isaiah 14:12–14 shares, "How you have fallen from heaven, morning star, son of the dawn! You have been cast down to the earth, you who once laid low the nations! You said in your heart, 'I will ascend to the heavens; I will raise my throne above the stars of God; I will sit enthroned on the mount of assembly, on the utmost heights of Mount Zaphon. I will ascend above the tops of clouds; I will make myself like the Most High.' " Revelation adds, "The great dragon was hurled down—that ancient serpent called

Where Do We Find Our Identity?

the devil, or Satan, who leads the whole world astray. He was hurled to the earth, and his angels with him. . . . He is filled with fury, because he knows that his time is short" (Revelation 12:9, 12).

Then he started an identity war here, too, when he tempted Adam and Eve and they sinned. There are so many distractions vying for our attention. Some are mentioned in Revelation 13:13, "And it performed great signs, even causing fire to come down from heaven to the earth in full view of the people." Distractions can easily become idolatry, replacing God's rightful place in our lives. Luke 4:5–7 shares that the devil wanted Jesus to worship him and in return he would give Jesus all the kingdoms of the world, "Jesus answered, 'It is written: "Worship the Lord your God and serve him only." ' " Jesus didn't worship Satan, but the devil has convinced many people to worship him. Revelation 13:8 shares, "All inhabitants of the earth will worship the beast—all whose names have not been written in the Lamb's book of life, the Lamb who was slain from the creation of the world." Let's turn our hearts and minds to Jesus and reject the distractions this world offers.

Grace reaches out first

Remember how God sent ten plagues to warn the Egyptians and deliver the children of Israel from slavery? The Israelites left Egypt, and the trip initially went smoothly until they reached the Red Sea. There, they discovered that they were caught between the sea, the mountains, and the approaching Egyptian army. Yet God had a plan in advance. His people needed to choose a new identity, because only going forward with God would work.

What did God say through Moses? Exodus records, "Moses answered the people, 'Do not be afraid. Stand firm and you will see the deliverance the Lord will bring you today. The Egyptians you see today you will never see again. The Lord will fight for you; you need only to be still' " (Exodus 14:13, 14). The Lord opened the sea for them to get out in a new direction. God's grace reached out, helped the Israelites escape, and filled their hearts with His peace. In return, the whole encampment broke out into song!

Prayer Still Moves Mountains

This reminds me of the time I was on a Women's Ministries Alaskan cruise ship for a mission trip with my friend Corleen. Daily we walked around and around the deck for exercise. When we reached the back of the ship, it always felt a little strange looking over the railing and down at the water. It's a steep drop-off! Have you ever looked over the railing at the back of a cruise ship? Sometimes people fall off or get thrown overboard. Suppose I fell overboard but I had faith that the ship's captain would see me and turn the ship around. Knowing that survival after falling in cold Alaskan water depends on being rescued within minutes—faith in a rescue isn't going to save me unless someone responds. Now if by God's grace the captain saw me, turned the boat around instantly, threw out a life jacket, and pulled me back on board in record time, then it wasn't anything I did to save me. Grace reached in and gave me my life back. Paul said it this way, "For it is by grace you have been saved through faith" (Ephesians 2:8). Notice, grace comes first—Jesus reached out first to cover our sin with His grace. John wrote, "My dear children, I write this to you so that you will not sin. But if anybody does sin, we have an advocate with the Father—Jesus Christ, the Righteous One. He is the atoning sacrifice for our sins, and not only for ours but also for the sins of the whole world" (1 John 2:1, 2). God reaches out to us with grace when we are floundering in sin and our sinful identity. He forgives our sins if we ask, and He remembers them no more. What do we want our identity to be? Will we accept God's grace covering our sins? Won't you join me in saying, "Yes, Lord we do! In Jesus, we are whole. By faith in Jesus, we are all good."

Reflection

1. Have you ever felt like you were thrown into the "blackberry bushes"? How did you get help after that? If you are still suffering from this, could you write down some ways God has shown you His love, either by illustration or through a Bible story?

2. Write out some personal "In Christ, I am _____" statements from Scripture.

Where Do We Find Our Identity?

3. What are some fruits of the Spirit you find helpful?

4. Say a prayer of thanks for God's grace reaching out to you.

---

1. "What Is Emotional Intelligence and How Does It Apply to the Workplace?" *Mental Health America,* accessed May 12, 2022, https://mhanational.org/what-emotional-intelligence-and-how-does-it-apply-workplace.

2. Dan Bray, "From the Counselor's Desk: Build Your EQ Starting Today," *For God & Country*, no. 4 (2020): 12.

Chapter 11

The Journey of God's Goodness

For everything that was written in the past was written to teach us, so that through the endurance taught in the Scriptures and the encouragement they provide we might have hope.

—Romans 15:4

One December day a few years ago, I received this email message from a friend: "This morning I realized something that is troubling me. Deep in my spirit and not just on a 'bad' day, but deep within, I struggle believing God is good. I can earnestly say, much of the time I genuinely doubt He is to me. Often I feel like He is indifferent or outright opposed. . . . I've just realized it this morning when I read God is good. I went, *Yeah, right. Not so much.* I'm not sure how to build that faith muscle?"

I wanted to respond. Partly because it hurt knowing someone didn't think that God was good. And partly because I wanted to see what I would say in response to the question about God's goodness. So I said a prayer and began.

> Dear friend, you ask about how to build a faith muscle about God's goodness. Many people have struggled with belief down through the ages, many not believing God is good at all. I have a short thought and also a longer one. Here's my short one: I think what has helped those who believe is faith

The Journey of God's Goodness

followed by action. Faith followed by action plants faith deep into our being. One tiny example is when I first moved into my neighborhood in the early 1990's. I would walk my road and pray. And I was certainly assailed by negative thoughts at the end of the road when I ran out of things to pray about. But one day, the idea came to me to praise God about the same pleas I had just prayed, and immediately the negative thoughts would dissipate. In the Christian walk there are two deaths: the belief in the death of Christ, and the death to self. And those are pivotal to understanding God's goodness.

Here's my longer answer, starting with a foundation from Genesis and including the death of Jesus and the death to self.

In the beginning, God created everything in six days and at the end of each day He called what He had made *good*. On the sixth day He saw all that He had made and called it *very good*. Then God created a Sabbath day, a memorial of Creation. He rested and called it holy. I imagine Him hiking around in awe of the beauty and splendor. Genesis 2 says God gave man a garden and all kinds of trees that were good for food (I hope even a dark-chocolate tree). There was a river that separated into four headwaters. First Corinthians 2:9 shares no mind can conceive what God has prepared for those who love Him. And the whole Creation story was good.

Adam and Eve had a face-to-face relationship with God, and they thought God was good until the devil planted the seed of doubt, "Did God really say?" Sometimes faith is the opposite of doubt. Cain, their son, teetered on the edge of doubt versus belief for a while. God saw that Cain was angry and tried to reason with him before he killed his brother (Genesis 4:6). But Cain resented that his sacrifice of fruit wasn't accepted, and he hated his brother Abel, who brought the specified sacrifice and received God's acceptance.

Prayer Still Moves Mountains

Abel exercised his faith "muscles" by believing God was good and then put action behind it with his sacrifice of a lamb as God had instructed. He had faith to reach for and claim the promised blessing before it was realized. Hebrews 11 calls Abel righteous. Like Abel, we send up our prayers and let our faith take hold of the promised blessing, and claim it as ours. When we believe, we receive it and according to God's word, it is ours. Faith rests on the promises in the Word of God, "If you remain in me and my words remain in you, ask whatever you wish, and it will be done for you" (John 15:7).

Down through the ages the devil has done much to destroy the belief that God is good. We all believe or disbelieve in varying degrees. The interesting thing about faith in Christ is that in order to truly believe God is good we trust two things. One, that Christ died for our sins. And two, we must die to self and start growing in Christ. Cain didn't die to self, he didn't care about the symbol of a lamb taking away his sins. His pride took over and he asked, "Isn't my sacrifice of fruit good enough?" His brother Abel put aside any thoughts of self. Instead, he used the sacrifice God called for and received God's blessing.

Blossoming from the inside

When we realize that Jesus has done the work of redemption for us, we relax from trying to earn our salvation through works and use the time to interact with and read about our Savior. We have heard the phrase, we become like those we spend time with. As we spend more time with Jesus versus spending time with people who don't like Jesus, we begin to grow and our life reflects attributes of the fruit of the Spirit. Galatians 5:22, 23 describes the fruit as "love, joy, peace, forbearance, kindness, goodness, faithfulness, gentleness and self-control."

The Journey of God's Goodness

Here's an example about death to self and growth in Jesus: "A seed germinates and the appearance of those first two leaves makes the gardener happy. A baby is born, and its first scream announces to the world that here is a new life to reckon with."[1] And what if, "Those leaves do not turn into four but rather remain the same or vanish away; a year later the little baby neither smiles nor takes a first step but remains frozen in the simplicity of its entrance into the world."[2]

Growing physically and spiritually is an inseparable factor of life. God has such patience with growth in His people and His church. We grow personally over time, and the church also grows over time. But throughout the growth process, the devil was and is there to throw in doubt through people and through church systems. In the dark ages, the Roman church didn't let the common people have the Bible that explained about God. They wanted to explain God through a system of rituals and, in some instances, bribes. The Reformation that resulted is an example of God working through people to restore the picture of who He is and how to relate to Him. Christian growth personally and corporately was supposed to continue as each new reformer over time profiled new principles of God's character and kingdom. What they profiled can be thought of as stepping-stones in the Christian faith. Taken as a whole, the beliefs they discovered by Bible study over time built a lovely picture of the God we serve, and these concepts are also what we can use to build our faith.

God loves us, the devil doesn't. He hates God because he can't be like Him. And we have seen plenty evidence of his hate. He was able to get people to misunderstand and hate Jesus, and then to kill Him. Now he hates God's people and turns them against each other. The love aspect of Christian growth is unique to the gospel. People love, but they love the loveable. Jesus introduces His plan, "A new command I give you: Love one another. As I have loved you, you must love one another" (John 13:34). This new love has no barrier, and it includes even enemies. Cain couldn't love his brother because he hadn't died to self and looked forward to Jesus' promises. As John wrote, "For if we don't love people we can see, how can we love God, whom we cannot see?" (1 John 4:20, NLT). I am thrilled that the ending of the book of Revelation ties up all the chaos and loose ends with paradise restored and living eternally with God and His goodness again. We get the garden and the fruit tree back, and the incredible river, and eternal joy!

Hope replaces worry

God daily reveals His goodness, but often we miss these demonstrations because we are distracted. For example, we can distract ourselves from seeing God's goodness by instead focusing on such burdens as worry, limitations, loneliness, hard choices, delays, losses, and guilt.

Many people are worried about something. Let's look at Abraham's story, beginning in Genesis 12, to see an example of how God works out the details of our lives. God started by calling him out to be separate from the world, and He pronounced a blessing on him for his journey. Genesis records, "The LORD had said to Abram, 'Go from your country, your people and your father's household to the land I will show you. I will make you into a great nation and I will bless you; I will make your name great, and you will be a blessing. I will bless those who bless you, and whoever curses you I will curse; and all peoples on earth will be blessed through you.' So Abram went" (Genesis 12:1–4).*

However, he soon encountered a famine: "Now there was a famine in the land" (verse 10). Abram had just heard God's promises of goodness and now he has to handle a test. How is Abram going to respond? Is Abram prepared to pass this test?

I'll never forget the day that my husband, Ron, came home with

---

* Later God changed Abram's name to Abraham (Genesis 17:5), and Sarai's name to Sarah (Genesis 17:15).

The Journey of God's Goodness

this long yellow tube in plastic wrap and handed it to me. He excitedly told me that it was an emergency rocket that I could keep in the truck and shoot up in the air if I was ever lost going over the mountain and out into the Oregon desert. I responded, "And if no one sees it in the air, then what?"

No reply.

Several months later in the winter, I found a long yellow webbing cord with hooks in the truck on the backseat floor. "Ron, what is the yellow webbing for?" I asked.

He responded, "Now you can tow people." I've never had to tow people in all my driving years, but I'm trying not to question these things in case it's a Holy Spirit thing. Because one day I may have to tow someone or shoot up a rocket. It's good to have them in advance, just in case.

Well, God is so good to us. He warns us that there is an emergency coming, and promises that if we prepare for His coming, we don't have to be worried. There is a lot of chaos, confusion, and trying times right now. Yet living in chaos is where "God moments" stand out. Otherwise, we might lose hope that God is with us in everything.

Somehow Abram was thrown off of remembering God's promises as he looked at the situation in front of him. Momentarily, Abram got distracted, and when he reached Egypt, he told Sarai to say she was his sister, and soon, Sarai was taken into Pharaoh's palace (verse 15). Thankfully, Abraham was still growing in his trust of God and God didn't hold this against him. Soon Sarai was returned unharmed. Later on, in Abraham's story, Abimelek said to Abraham, "God is with you in everything you do" (Genesis 21:22). This is a great promise to claim for our lives as we grow in our trust of God too.

Several years ago, I was doing Bible studies with a woman whose name I received from an *It Is Written* interest list. As we studied, I noticed that the woman often seemed anxious about unresolved issues. After taking her to some evangelistic meetings by Shawn Boonstra, she wanted to see more of Shawn's presentations. One day I rushed out the door for the study; however, when I arrived at her complex, I realized

Prayer Still Moves Mountains

I didn't have a DVD with me. I said a quick prayer. *Lord help me! Now what do You want me to do?*

I walked in, chatted a few moments, and admitted, "I forgot the DVD. However, in my Bible, I do have sixteen little Bible studies complete with the texts that go with them. We could look at one of those."

"What are they?" she asked as I showed her the listing. She chose the first one, a study on the Word of God. I started with a prayer for the Holy Spirit to guide us, and we began.

As we read through several verses, she suddenly had a "God moment" as she read Paul's words, "For everything that was written in the past was written to teach us, so that through endurance and the encouragement of the Scriptures we might have hope" (Romans 15:4).

"That's what I need! I need hope!" she suddenly exclaimed. "Every day I read for two hours, and I start with all these books that people have given me to try to help my anxiety. After about two hours I am too tired to open the Bible. Maybe I should start with the Bible first."

What a revelation! I thought, and what a praise this turned out to be. God knew that starting with Him and His Scriptures first would bring her the hope she needed.

Since God has all these details figured out, what are we worried about? Hope replaces worry. I once had two dogs named Twister and Flash. Twister wanted to live in the house 24-7. If it looked as though we were getting ready to go somewhere, she would run and hide under the bed. Flash would continue squeaking his toy and wanting to play. Twister would hide under the bed thinking impending doom was coming while Flash was oblivious and continued to have fun. But Twister sometimes worried for hours needlessly.

Perplexities can vanish

The author Ellen White shares in *The Desire of Ages*,

> There are many whose hearts are aching under a load of care because they seek to reach the world's standard. They

The Journey of God's Goodness

have chosen its service, accepted its perplexities, adopted its customs. Thus their character is marred, and their life made a weariness. In order to gratify ambition and worldly desires, they wound the conscience, and bring upon themselves an additional burden of remorse. The continual worry is wearing out the life forces. Our Lord desires them to lay aside this yoke of bondage. He invites them to accept His yoke; He says, "My yoke is easy, and My burden is light." He bids them seek first the kingdom of God and His righteousness, and His promise is that all things needful to them for this life shall be added. Worry is blind, and cannot discern the future; but Jesus sees the end from the beginning. In every difficulty He has His way prepared to bring relief. Our heavenly Father has a thousand ways to provide for us, of which we know nothing. Those who accept the one principle of making the service and honor of God supreme will find perplexities vanish, and a plain path before their feet.[3]

God's goodness never ends

A few days after I had written to my friend about God's goodness, I thought that I was done with writing about God's goodness. Then on December 16 a package was delivered to the house, and I realized that God wanted to make it a continuous journey. The package was from Nicole, a woman I met in Texas that past June when I spoke at the Keene camp meeting. Nicole was a really nice woman who drove me around when I needed a ride. One day, we went on a walk together and shared about our lives. The package she sent contained a prayer journal. I have to admit I did a small double take at first since I usually write everything on my computer. As I thought about how to best use it, the thought came to me, *It is almost the beginning of the year. I could go through the alphabet and choose a word for each letter describing a characteristic of God's goodness and write about it.* And I would also pray for people whose names began with those letters. Thank you, Nicole, for your wonderful gift.

Prayer Still Moves Mountains

I wasn't sure what to do for A. So I just reached for the thesaurus and opened to A words and saw the word "Arms." *I love the picture of the Lord's arms around me through life. Upholding and reassuring me as if in a warm embrace.* The next day was easier, I knew that we wouldn't know about the Lord's goodness without the Bible, and I prayed for a relative whose name starts with a B.

Journaling about God's character for each letter of the alphabet was a helpful example to me of faith followed by action. It is good to look back and remember what the Lord has done for us. It strengthens and encourages us going forward.

Even Job thought God was good

On February 9, 2019, we received three inches of snow during the night. Several churches sent out a notice that they were not having church. But Ron and I took his mom, Ruth, to Hood View Church because they were open. Ron wandered over to the info desk and then waved me over. "Look at this, they are doing something called a Bible Experience. It says during the new year church members are encouraged to read three chapters each day and someone will write a devotional about it. They write these ahead, post them online, and also print some out for people to read. You should sign up to write one."

I agreed, and looked at the sign-up sheet. As I glanced at the chapter possibilities, I decided Job 38, 39, and Psalm 145 would be good. I knew Job 38 is where God starts asking questions after listening to Job's three friends discuss his suffering. He describes how immense He is, so He must be good!

The next day, I received instructions and the request that I turn it in by February 24. So I began writing:

> God, in effusive writing describing His own goodness, also has trouble being concise. In Job 38 God answered Job and his friends after hearing them ramble much about reasons Job was suffering. God overwhelmed them with many questions impossible for humans to answer. Verse 4, NIV, asks,

The Journey of God's Goodness

"Where were you when I laid the earth's foundation? Tell me, if you understand." Verse 33 inquires, "Do you know the laws of the heavens? Can you set up God's dominion over the earth?" It appears God is trying to say we will never comprehend what He knows. In agreement, it would be good to trust Him with the details of our lives. Sometimes when I have wondered at God's goodness, He has given me little reminders throughout the day.

Psalm 145:13 shares that "the Lord is trustworthy in all he promises and faithful in all he does." I have discovered in life that faith followed by action helps with belief. It's a joy to continue sharing about God's goodness and how He has helped me in life. It strengthens my understanding that He is good.[4]

God rewrites Abraham's story

It is interesting that when Abraham chose to hope in God instead of listening to his fears, God rewrote his story to say that he "in hope believed" and "without weakening in faith," was credited with righteousness. Note that we also are credited with righteousness. Romans 4:18–25 counsels,

> Against all hope, Abraham in hope believed and so became the father of many nations, just as it had been said to him, "So shall your offspring be." Without weakening in his faith, he faced the fact that his body was as good as dead—since he was about a hundred years old—and that Sarah's womb was also dead. Yet he did not waver through unbelief regarding the promise of God, but was strengthened in his faith and gave glory to God, being fully persuaded that God had power to do what he had promised. This is why "it was credited to him as righteousness." The words "it was credited to him" were written not for him alone, but also for us, to whom God will credit righteousness—for us who believe in him who raised Jesus our Lord from the dead. He was delivered

over to death for our sins and was raised to life for our justification.

How's that for a good God!

The actions of God reflect God's goodness
A couple days later, I was in the dollar store looking for a card and small gift for someone. My eyes fell on a little book called *Goodness (Nine Fruits of the Spirit),* by Robert Strand. As I flipped it over, I realized they were making a book out of each of the nine fruits of the spirit. And this was the one devoted to goodness. Galatians 5:22, 23 shares, "But the fruit of the spirit is love, joy, peace, forbearance, kindness, goodness, faithfulness, gentleness and self-control."

This book was just for me! I drove home to read, and then called someone to try out the questions the book suggested. I asked the person to "describe what you mean by calling someone a good person." And they described a good person.

Then this question, "Would you consider yourself a good person? Why? or Why not?" And they described why they were a good person.

The book had me read about God's goodness in Psalm 100:1–5 (take a moment to read that if you wish). Then I asked, "What do we know about the character of God from Psalm 100?" And they answered.

Then came the next question: "Exactly how do we know that God is good?"

They responded, "I don't know that God is good."

I was stymied. After sharing how people were good, the individual thought they were good, and hearing Psalm 100, they didn't think God was good. There are so many reasons people don't believe God is good. Here's a few from a former atheist named Vince Antonucci. Online I found that he shares, "When faced with unanswerable questions, a person can assume the faith they believe in is inadequate or irrelevant."[5] And, "Some turn because God didn't answer an important prayer or rescue them from the consequences of a bad decision. They may have been hurt by a church or turned off by hypocritical Christians. One

The Journey of God's Goodness

study found that many of the most well-known atheists grew up without a father."[6]

The next question I decided to ask of myself, "How do the actions of God reflect the goodness of God?" Personally, I see God's goodness in my life in lining up the details of my life, giving me family and friends to spend time with, a whole day to set apart with Jesus on the Sabbath, and giving me "God moment" surprises. Acts 10:38 also has a perfect answer. Peter describes Jesus as good. He shares, "How God anointed Jesus of Nazareth with the Holy Spirit and power, and how he went around doing good and healing all who were under the power of the devil, because God was with him."

Time to reflect about God's goodness
Here is one example of time spent with God and a friend where God's actions to us portrayed His character of being good. It was April 20, 2018, and I set out for a mini prayer retreat in Sunriver with my friend Linda. We stopped in Sisters for a yummy lunch at Angeline's Bakery and Cafe, toured a couple shops, and then we headed to hike the Metolius River. April can still be cold and rainy in eastern Oregon, so we asked God to hold the clouds and rain back. It was delightful to see blue butterflies fly up in front of us as we stepped near. Next, we drove to a fish hatchery and stared deeply into the incredible blue water—with patches resembling both azure and sapphire colors. We walked partway around the small lake at the fish hatchery and then sat on a bench to pray. Just as we were closing our eyes, I noticed two Canada geese in the middle of the lake start to swim toward us. I kept my eyes open during prayer as the geese reached us, got out, and walked up to the grass beside us and started eating.

"Oh, look at that," Linda exclaimed as she opened her eyes. "We have geese right beside us." Moments later the sun went behind the clouds, and it suddenly felt cold. *This is another reminder of God's goodness—I'll have to record this in my journal*, I thought. Watching how God works when we take time away is one of my favorite reasons to take a retreat.

Prayer Still Moves Mountains

"This has been such a blessing to me," I shared with Linda the next morning. "We should invite other ladies to enjoy a retreat here."

"Diane, moments ago I was downstairs thinking the same thing. It seems like a God thing that you would say that," she replied. "We could make the emphasis a mini health retreat where they learn some healthy cooking, exercises, and facts about brain health. I have learned a lot of tips from Neil Nedley's *Optimize Your Brain* program. In fact, we just had it at our church."

"Oh, I am excited now. Let's pray about the plan," I suggested.

Reflection

1. Take a moment trying to describe God's goodness by sharing a remembrance of a time the Lord did something for you. Thank Him for His goodness.

2. Consider compiling verses that describe God's goodness.

3. Study Romans 4:18–25 and reflect on the process it takes to be "credited [with] righteousness."

---

1. *Seventh-day Adventists Believe* (Silver Spring, MD: Review and Herald®, 2018), 151.
2. *Seventh-day Adventists Believe*, 151.
3. Ellen G. White, *The Desire of Ages* (Nampa, ID: Pacific Press®, 2005), 330.
4. Diane Pestes, "Job 38–39; Psalm 145," Bible Experience, May 30, 2019, https://www.hoodviewbible.com/blog/2018/12/28/job24-pw8aw-3e5p4-6pg43-z8zgd?rq=diane%20pestes.
5. Vince Antonucci, "Nine Reasons People Don't Believe in God," *City on a Hill*, accessed April 5, 2022, https://cityonahillstudio.com/9-reasons-people-dont-believe-god/.
6. Antonucci, "Nine Reasons."

Chapter 12

Crowding Out the "Bad" With the "Good"

*"But I will restore you to health and heal your wounds,"
declares the* L*ord*.

—Jeremiah 30:17

After prayer, my friend Linda and I immediately started chatting about the potential health retreat weekend. I asked, "Linda, where are we going to find women who want to come for a health retreat? I think it should be for ladies who really need to know the information. Not just those who want to go to Sunriver."

"I think we should give first priority to those who attended the 'Optimize Your Brain' class at church and this can be a follow-up weekend. After that, we can invite ladies who attend my exercise class that I teach at Coastal Fitness. I will put the idea out there and ask. Some of those at the gym are not interested in things like attending a church and some study mind, body and spirit practices. However, most people, and especially the latter group, are really interested in health," Linda replied.

"That's a good idea! I will also ask my friend Sandy that I walk with on my road. She always seems interested in health. Maybe she has some friends."

Crowding out the "bad" with the "good"
After deciding that June would be a good month to host our health

weekend, Linda and I began making plans. One day during a call, Linda shared, "I am looking through my recipe books to see which healthful recipes to teach. I want to give them many options to crowd out the less healthy options people usually eat."

"That sounds like a good idea. I made a promo piece and mini schedule with some pictures of vegetables, pasta salad, and eggplant. I'll email that to you, and I can check into getting passes for the pool if we want to take a couple hours to exercise there," I replied.

"I'm sure some women would want to use the pool," she assured me. Then we uplifted the health retreat in prayer again.

The next day while walking with Sandy, I shared about the upcoming health retreat. "We are going to have cooking demonstrations, and Linda will guide participants while they make the recipes. There will be a time for walking and swimming. We will also watch some DVDs on health, and afterward Linda can answer questions."

"I want to go, and I'm sure my friend Kathy would want to go too. What would we need to bring?" Sandy asked.

"There is a fee that covers the food. We have enough beds and towels for everyone. Bring a swimsuit if you want to swim, because we'll have an exercise break Friday afternoon after the cooking class," I responded.

"I'm looking forward to this," she said.

"Me too," I replied.

Soon we had six women signed-up, and with Linda and myself that made eight. This was a good size because eight ladies in a kitchen at one time is quite a handful. God brought a wide variety of women together for this weekend, and most of the group came from the Linda's exercise class.

Thursday, June 7, Linda went over early to shop for ingredients in Bend, Oregon. The rest of the group arrived later that evening because we had a full schedule planned beginning first thing Friday morning.

We began each day with a gathering time that was similar to a morning devotional. Then we did a half hour of easy Pilates exercises—it felt good to loosen up! Linda wanted to make all of our food for Friday night and Sabbath ahead of time so we wouldn't have to cook

Crowding Out the "Bad" With the "Good"

on Sabbath, just warm some things up. This plan worked well—seven ladies in the kitchen making separate recipes while Linda observed and gave suggestions. Then we had lunch, and four of us went swimming while the others stayed at the house to connect and take a walk.

During each meal Linda would chat about a few health tips. It made for some pretty interesting conversations with the diverse group. At the Friday evening meal, someone commented to Linda what a blessing it must be to know all this information, and asked how long she had known it?

She surprised them by saying, "I didn't grow up eating healthy like this, and how I came to is a long story. Someday I'll share it. I really like crowding out the bad foods by eating healthfully. And I find when I present people with good recipes, then they use those instead of less nutrient dense ones."

"Please share your story," they replied. "We want to hear it."

"We don't have time for it since we have another health DVD to watch. I really don't want you to miss out on those," she shared. However, God had other plans. Linda and I prayed downstairs before the next meeting, and when we came upstairs to start we could not get the DVD player to work, at all. It had worked for the afternoon meeting, but wouldn't work now.

Then Sandy suggested, "Well, maybe we are supposed to hear your testimony instead."

"All right, I will share some of my story," Linda replied.

The "God spot"

Linda began, "Like Pascal, I believe that in each of us there is a 'God spot.' It is the spot that only God can fill. No matter how hard we try to fill this spot it will never be satisfied until we know God personally—unless we surrender our life to Him. Until we know God is love, and we allow Him to dwell in us.

"As a child I wasn't raised in a Christian family. My family was a wonderful family, but I was never given any instruction about God. I can remember wondering at times when I was young if there was a God.

Prayer Still Moves Mountains

But I never gave the subject much thought. In my adolescent years, I felt very insecure and wondered at times, why am I me? Would I ever be married and have children? *Well,* I thought, *if I were taller, thinner, smarter, and more attractive maybe, yes, I would possibly get married, raise a family, and live happily ever after.* At this time in my life my insecurity was at times overwhelming. I felt a deep need to be accepted and loved, as do many young people at this age. This need seemed fulfilled in a relationship with a young man. I could see myself one day married to him and raising a family. Things were wonderful, until the relationship turned toxic and I realized that for my own safety and sanity I needed to end the relationship. The decision was heartbreaking to me, and in my great pain and through tear-filled eyes I looked into the sky one night and cried out, 'God, if You're real, show me.'

"As it turns out, I ended up marrying the friend of my youngest uncle, 'my knight in shining armor,' I called him. He was seven years older than me and so much more mature than the young man I thought I would spend my life with. He had served in the military and had seen the world. Surely we would have the perfect life together. We soon found out that neither of us were perfect, so once again the perfect marriage looked beyond my reach. Our marriage took a turn for the worse when I saw our partying and drinking as a way to escape my unhappiness from a not-so-happy marriage. Things quickly spiraled out of control, and I wanted a divorce. About that time, a friend of my husband gave him a book called *The Late Great Planet Earth*. It was a book about end-time events and Jesus' second coming. The friend told my husband, George, he would be praying for us. When George brought it home, he asked me to read it, and I told him, 'No. I don't want anything to do with it.' God was the farthest thing from my mind. Read a book about God? No way.

"George laid the book down in front of me and went to bed. But I was in a state of agitation and restlessness and couldn't sleep. After much internal struggle I picked up the book and began to read. In the beginning I read out of curiosity, but before long it turned from curiosity into interest. Soon I was reading with a deep fear that what

Crowding Out the "Bad" With the "Good"

I was reading might be true. It talked about before Jesus comes the second time there would be wars, earthquakes, pestilence, famines, which would get worse and worse. It compared these events to birth pangs before a woman delivers a child. I could identify with that since I had a five-year-old and a two-year-old. I began to think that if what I was reading was true and there was a God, then I would be going to hell. As I read, I began to question whether the author was correctly applying the Bible verses to the points he made and his overall view of prophecy. We didn't own a Bible, but now I had a desire to get a Bible and read it for myself to discover if what I was reading was correct. Later, when I mentioned not having a Bible to my mother-in-law, she rushed to another room and brought a Bible out. It was a Bible my husband used as a child when he went to catechism for a brief time. I could hardly wait to get home and dig in and check for myself if the book I had been reading was correctly applying the Bible in his interpretation of prophecy. I quickly discovered he was correct about the fact that all the signs happening around me pointed to the end of the world and Jesus' second coming. But I found that other things were not lining up with what the Bible said.

"The book showed me how to accept Jesus into my heart and be born again. It said we are all sinners and we can be saved only by the sacrifice and blood of Jesus. And if we confess our sins, He is faithful and just to forgive us our sins and cleanse us of all unrighteousness (1 John 1:9). I began confessing, asking forgiveness, and asking Jesus to lead and guide me in my life. As I fell to the floor, I cried and cried and felt the Holy Spirit enter my life. When I rose to my feet, I felt like a new person—life was different from that moment on. I finally felt deeply loved and accepted by the Creator and Redeemer of my soul. For two years I prayed and studied my Bible, asking God to lead me to a fellowship teaching prophecy and health. And He did just that—I was led to the Seventh-day Adventist Church. My husband and I attended a prophecy seminar and later became Seventh-day Adventists. Satan did everything possible to prevent us from making that commitment, but God prevailed in our lives. It was a new beginning for our family.

Prayer Still Moves Mountains

George and I have since celebrated our fiftieth wedding anniversary.

"Since joining the Seventh-day Adventist Church, God has given me a deep love and understanding of prophecy and the blessed hope of Jesus' second coming. I am so thankful to have learned a new way of eating and caring for my body—health principles to boost my immune system for such a time as this.

"God replaced friendships that were destructive with friendships that have encouraged me in my walk with the Lord. Habits that were destructive, with habits that are constructive and for the building up of my body temple and those around me. God has given me opportunities to share what He has taught me, such as mission trips to share Jesus and what He's done in my life. He has given me opportunities to encourage my sisters in Christ and share my love of Jesus. And also cooking classes—to share how to build up the body temple through God's original diet. Jesus fulfills every desire in our heart, and each day is a new beginning.

"I have found the answer to my first desperate prayer that I had years before cried out, *God if You're real, show me.* He has given me many evidences that He is *very* real. I was reminded of Moses' prayer in Exodus 33:13, 'If I have found grace in thy sight, shew me now thy way, that I may know thee' (KJV). Soon after the Lord descended in a cloud and stood with Moses and proclaimed His name. I am truly blessed that as I look back over my life I can see how God brought me from an attitude of hopelessness to understanding that my future and hope comes from loving and being loved by Jesus. I wish that everyone could see what a difference Jesus makes. The Bible tells how God created man in His image. The Scripture also tells us that 'God is love.' So Adam must have reflected the love of God. First John 4:16 says, 'God is love; and he that dwelleth in love dwelleth in God, and God in him' (KJV). Essentially, we were created to love and be loved by Him.

"Since the Fall, something drastically changed in regard to love. Instead of Godlike love dwelling in man it became perverted. Oh, man still desired love, but it was now self-serving. Unlike God's unfailing

Crowding Out the "Bad" With the "Good"

love, man's love was dependent on his feelings. The attitude is, 'If you make me happy, doing things, saying things that make me feel good, then you are worthy of my love. If not, I can no longer love you.' Jesus came to reveal what true love looks like. As He hung on the cross beaten, bleeding, and ready to die, His words, 'Father, forgive them for they know not what they do,' reveal what God's love looks like. And when we ask for that love, our life begins anew."

Linda then shared some reference verses for a study on how the universe started and a description of God's love: Genesis 1:26, 27; Genesis 1:31; 1 John 4:7, 8; Genesis 2:16, 17; Genesis 3:4, 5; Genesis 3:6; Genesis 3:8; and Genesis 3:9, 10.

Hugging trees to prayer

Sabbath afternoon during the break, the ladies who focus on the mind, body and spirit, joined us and explained they had just returned from hugging a tree and felt renewed energy from that. Linda and I had been praying that they would recognize God in what was presented. As Linda knew from conversations at the gym, the women believe that physical objects, such as trees or other objects, have a presence of spiritual energy. And we wanted to direct them to the Creator instead. The experience was a good reminder of Romans 1:25, "They exchanged the truth about God for a lie, and worshiped and served created things rather than the Creator—who is forever praised. Amen."

We hoped instead to crowd out the bad with the good, as Paul counseled in Philippians 4:8, "Finally, brothers and sisters, whatever is true, whatever is noble, whatever is right, whatever is pure, whatever is lovely, whatever is admirable—if anything is excellent or praiseworthy—think about such things."

By the end of the weekend, we were able to chat separately with those who had hugged trees about a couple of misconceptions, and they requested prayer over their lives. Another woman stated a desire for a closer relationship with Christ. So many good conversations happened that weekend.

Prayer Still Moves Mountains

The breaded eggplant recipe

Standing in the produce section of the grocery store, I stared at the eggplants. Linda had said, "Look for a darker one that gives slightly when you push into it." As I grabbed one that seemed darker, I noticed two people were standing close to me, and the man was sharing thoughts about another vegetable. Intrigued at his comments, I held out the eggplant and asked, "Would you say that this eggplant is ripe?"

"Let me compare it with some others," he responded, and took the eggplant from me and turned to the other eggplants. His wife then asked, "What are you going to do with the eggplant?"

"I'm making gluten-free breaded eggplant. It's really tasty." I tried to remember my recipe card that I had glanced over and left in the truck, and continued, "You peel them, slice lengthwise, and dip in whizzed garbanzo beans with equal parts of water. Then dip in either corn flakes that you crushed into a powder or use nutritional yeast flakes then bake it."

"What temperature do you use?" she asked.

"350 degrees," I replied.

"I'm going to try this," she responded. Just then her husband came around and stood in front of us with two eggplants and said, "Feel these and see if you notice which one would be better. This is the one you had."

"Hmm, mine is a little too soft. This one feels better," I replied.

"Right," he affirmed.

"Thank you for your help," I said and turned to his wife. "Have fun with the casserole."

Correct directions are helpful

"You left out the spices. And I would put the cornflakes and yeast flakes together," Linda responded when I told her later that I was excited to be in the grocery section and share how to make breaded eggplant with a perfect stranger.

"Oh no, and I had the recipe in the truck! I almost went out to get it. She might not like her eggplant as much," I replied.

Crowding Out the "Bad" With the "Good"

"And I usually broil mine for five minutes and then flip it over and zigzag on a little spaghetti sauce and broil another five minutes. So hers might be a little too limp," Linda said. We both had a little laugh that directions could be messed up so easily. In my defense, I hadn't made that eggplant recipe before, just watched others making it. After getting even more tips, I made it for my mom, and we both loved it. It feels good to eat healthful and try to crowd out the bad by using the good. This can apply in all aspects of our lives—we in turn can focus on the good instead of the bad. And let us never forget that God will soon get rid of sin and re-create the world to be perfect again.

Reflection

1. If you have recognized a need to crowd out something you are doing with something that is better, please make a commitment to do that. Perhaps call a friend to share what you will be doing and pray together. When we share with others, it helps us keep on track.

2. Find other Scripture verses that talk about healthier options for our lives and journal about them or commit them to memory.

3. Consider reading all the "In the beginning" verses from Linda's testimony section and share with others about God's character of love (Genesis 1:26, 27; Genesis 1:31; 1 John 4:7, 8; Genesis 2:16, 17; Genesis 3:4, 5; Genesis 3:6; Genesis 3:8; and Genesis 3:9, 10).

Chapter 13

Something That Lasts

And I heard a loud voice from the throne saying, "Look! God's dwelling place is now among the people, and he will dwell with them. They will be his people, and God himself will be with them and be their God. 'He will wipe every tear from their eyes. There will be no more death' or mourning or crying or pain, for the old order of things has passed away."
—Revelation 21:3, 4

"You should probably go visit your grandmother," my dad told me over the phone.

Later that day, I drove to the Mt. St. Joseph Care Center in Portland, Oregon, to see my grandma. It was June 22, 2003, and I was glad that Grandma's courage seemed strong. The day before, she had told my parents that she just wanted to close her eyes and go to sleep and wake up to see Jesus. She only wanted them to talk about Jesus.

During our visit she said to me, "I just want God's will to be done, and maybe He is not done with me yet. He keeps bringing me little things to help me."

"Indeed," I said. "You are still needed here. Maybe God is still using you to pray for others."

She replied, "Maybe I can help someone."

As I sat with her, I remembered a time when I visited my grandmother during my childhood. I had curled up beside my grandmother that night, and my grandma told me a story. She said, "There is a huge

Something That Lasts

stack of rice in a barn, and there is an ant that approaches the rice and grabs a piece and takes it to another building. Then he comes back and grabs another piece and walks off toward the other building and sets it down. Then the little ant comes back and grabs another piece and walks off toward the other building and sets it down. Then the little ant comes back and grabs another piece and walks off toward the other building and sets it down."

Not at all sleepy, I asked her, "Why can't the ant get help so he can get the job done?" It really bugged me that he never finished his task and that he didn't delegate some of the work to his friends. Then I lay awake irritated, and finally asked for another story—but my grandmother had fallen asleep!

Coming back to the present, I turned to her for reassurance of the better story to come and observed, "I sure look forward to Jesus coming to take us to heaven, don't you?"

"Yes, I want to see my whole family in heaven. And this includes my brothers and sisters and parents. They lived a good Christian life," she said. "I look forward to being with my loved ones forever and ever—God's promise brings contentment and assurance. I prayed for all my friends for years, and I think most of them finally accepted Jesus. I pray for all my family, including grandsons and granddaughters."

I replied, "That's a lot of names to remember."

It reminds me of all the begats in the Bible, you know, "Abraham was the father of Isaac, Isaac the father of Jacob, Jacob the father of Judah and his brothers, Judah the father of Perez and Zerah, whose mother was Tamar," and so on (Matthew 1:2).

My grandma sure did her part in begetting of children—nine sons and daughters—who begat more sons and daughters who begat more . . . well, you get the picture. She loved them all.

A few weeks later, July 21, 2003, she was residing at my uncle's house surrounded by sons, daughters, and their spouses. She lifted up her hands and said, "I need Thee. I need Thee."

When asked, "Who?"

She replied, "Jesus." Those were her final words.

Prayer Still Moves Mountains

How I look forward to being reunited with her in heaven and hearing more of her stories and making more memories with her.

Too young

At times it felt as though I had been praying for my cousin Debi my whole life. I always looked up to her because she was five years older than me. When my brother and I went to stay at Grandma's house, Debi would often be there too. But then, when I was seven, she suddenly disappeared from my life along with two other cousins after their parents divorced and her mother took them to live back East. This troubled me greatly, and I remember praying for years that God would fix it. When Debi turned eighteen, she flew out to see us. I was thirteen, and I remember proudly sitting in the front seat with her as she drove home from a family picnic. I still looked up to her and eagerly looked forward to more visits. And I continued to pray for her. Eventually she married and had children, and came out West a few times to visit.

Then in 2002, Ron and I went back East to see the sights, and we stayed with Debi. She excitedly showed us her farm, her remodeling project upstairs, and her numerous outdoor projects. We had a lovely visit, and because our visits were so few and far between, I found it hard to leave. The next year I was horrified to learn that she'd been kicked in the head by her horse, and one of the long-term side effects of the accident was a lingering depression.

Several times I reached out by phone to chat and pray with her, but it was hard. Her family fell apart, she wanted to give up, and she questioned her faith in God. The struggle to reconcile the reality of the difficulties we face here on earth with the Bible's description of God's goodness and care is not uncommon. At the time, Debi was caught in the middle of a fierce battle between God and the devil. It's the custody battle we all face during this lifetime. Satan works to claim us as his, yet God demonstrated His love and power at the cross and Jesus' resurrection and calls us to follow Him. Ephesians 6:12 reminds us, "For our struggle is not against flesh and blood, but against the

Something That Lasts

rulers, against the authorities, against the powers of this dark world and against the spiritual forces of evil in the heavenly realms."

Then, in April 2004, Corleen and I took an opportunity to go back East and visit with Ginger Church, the director of the *Women of Spirit* magazine, at some meetings. The meetings were canceled, but Ginger urged us to come anyway—and it turned out to be providential. Before arriving at Ginger's house, we worked in a visit to Georgia Shaffer in Pennsylvania then traveled the next day to Westminster, Maryland, on April 23. My cousin Debi met us at our Days Inn hotel and then drove us to the local Olive Garden. She burst into tears as she told us of her situation. Life seemed hopeless to her, and she was desperate for her ex-husband to take their children because she had given up. This spoke volumes to me of the level of her depression because past experience taught me that Debi would never wish to give her children away. After we ate, we returned to our hotel and prayed with Debi. Before she left, we encouraged Debi to meet us the next day at the Westminster Seventh-day Adventist Church.

After Debi left, I turned to Corleen and said with a heavy heart, "We didn't do anything. How was that helpful?"

"Yes, we did," she replied, "We listened to her, and then we invited her to church."

The next day Debi met us at the Westminster Seventh-day Adventist Church. People were instantly drawn to her ready smile and warmth, and the shadow that had hung over her the day before seemed abated. She appeared to be a little better. Her cell phone rang in the middle of church, and she leaned over in the pew. "Hello honey. Where am I? I'm in church. No, I did say church. I'm in church. I know it is a Saturday. But it's an Adventist church and they meet on Saturdays." By now everyone could hear her conversation, and as I glanced around I could tell they didn't mind. During prayer time, they prayed for Debi after she raised her hand. Then we washed each other's feet at Communion. It was a special time. We ate potluck together, and they promised to call her soon. She told them, "I'll see you next Sabbath." I couldn't believe my ears. It sounded as though she had mustered some

Prayer Still Moves Mountains

courage and hope, and was turning a corner.

After a yummy potluck, we went to Debi's home and sat outside visiting. Then we read some from the Bible and prayed for continued peace and healing. Afterward we floated in paddle boats on her pond and she exclaimed, "I haven't done this in two years!"

We were excited that her spirits had lifted over the course of twenty-four hours. It was clear that Debi's heart was sensitive toward God. When we went into her house that Sabbath afternoon, she pointed to her kitchen wall and said, "See, here is the text that you mailed me. I look at it every morning." I don't remember now what verse it was, but I grew excited because she was excited.

Now I cling to Scripture promises and remember our time together during that special visit as I look forward to seeing her again in heaven—because a year and several months later she took her life. Revelation 21:4 assures, "And God will wipe away every tear from their eyes; there shall be no more death, nor sorrow, nor crying. There shall be no more pain, for the former things have passed away" (NKJV). And Isaiah 32:18 encourages, "My people will live in peaceful dwelling places, in secure homes, in undisturbed places of rest."

Revived for "better closure"

"Ron, the doctor just said Neil died on the surgery table. They have been doing CPR on his heart for 40 minutes. The doctor came out to ask me if I want them to continue pumping, and I told them no," Ron's mother, Ruth, related over the phone. Days before, Ron's father had fallen and broken his hip, and they were now doing surgery.

At the instant I heard Ruth tell Ron "—if I want them to continue pumping, and I told them no," I cried out to God, "If You need Neil to live, right now put Your hand on his heart and sustain him!"

Ron and I rushed to the hospital and arrived in time to hear the doctor say, "I walked back into surgery to tell them to stop pumping. When they stopped, his heart started pumping by itself."

They didn't finish the surgery. They just closed the wound and sent him to the intensive care unit. When we entered the unit, Ruth stood

Something That Lasts

on one side of Neil and motioned me in. She turned to Neil and said, "Neil, Diane is here, and she is going to say a prayer for you."

In my head I thought, *How should I pray? This is all so sudden and awful.* I don't remember most of my prayer that day, but I do remember asking God to send a "God moment" during this time.

Next, we had a flurry of family gathering outside the ICU doors and then a meeting with the doctor about what should happen next. Since Neil's hip wasn't fixed, it was decided that the doctor would wait a few days till Neil was stable enough for another surgery to fix his hip. Many people were in the waiting room with Ruth for Neil's second surgery. We were not sure Neil would make it through the surgery and had given instructions to not pump his heart if it stopped. One of the reasons for this was because the doctor informed us that his heart was down to twenty percent function because of congestive heart failure.

Ruth said, "I wasn't ready yesterday, but I think I'm ready today if I lose him."

I replied, "Yes, we have God, guardian angels, and church family, as well as our family to help us."

This time Neil sailed through the surgery and was eventually sent to a regular room. He rallied for several days and then started to take a turn downward.

One day, Ruth and a couple family members visited Neil, but he was asleep the whole time. They went to lunch, and when they returned, it wasn't long before he exhaled and didn't take another breath.

Later, I received a phone call from my friend Pam, a chaplain at the hospital, who shared a story with me. Pam related that while she was doing rounds on Neil's floor, she suddenly felt impressed that she needed to go to his room. She knew from her list that he wasn't doing well. When she stepped in, he was awake and by himself. She asked him about his relationship with God. He gave a mini testimony about his life journey with God and that he was assured of salvation and had peace. She had a prayer with him and then left. When Ruth and family returned, he was asleep again, and then he fell asleep till Jesus comes. It is amazing what can happen when no one is looking. But

Prayer Still Moves Mountains

God knows and doesn't forget us, and He sends a God moment when we need them most.

Weary for something that lasts

In 2017 my dad had been on hospice for two years, and during August he went into a respite care facility for five days while my mom took a break. Hospice called the evening before he was to return home and said that my dad had taken a turn for the worse. When I arrived, I saw that my dad was slumped in a chair and looked very out of it. My brother, Mark, arrived soon after me.

Two hospice nurses were there, and one shared, "I don't think that Marion will make it till morning. Something happened at the respite care home and his body gave out, maybe a liver, since his eyes are now very yellow and his body is yellow." We had gotten used to his body being slightly yellow though and didn't think much about it.

I was able to sit by my dad, and I soothed, "Dad, Jesus is going to make everything better soon." That was all I could choke out. Oh, how I long for something that lasts!

The next morning my mom called me and said, "I think he's gone."

"I'll be right over," I replied.

My mom said she had gone into my dad's room around three in the morning to check on him and he was still breathing. Then she went in at about 8:30 A.M. and he was not breathing. He had just quietly passed away. This was an answer to my prayers that he wouldn't suffer at the end. I stayed with my mom for a while and called some family and friends to share the news.

The next day my mom and I went to the funeral home to make arrangements. The funeral director went over a lot of information, and there were many details to be decided. One was whether we wanted a spray of flowers on top of the casket after the flag was taken off. It would cost more than two hundred dollars.

I was horrified at the thought of my mom shouldering that expense and asked, "Could we do something else instead?"

"You can do whatever you wish," the funeral director replied.

Something That Lasts

So I suggested that my nephew step forward with my dad's Bible and place it on the casket.

Shortly after that the director mentioned a package that included a guest book and programs. I said, "If the programs are going to cost a lot, then we will have to go without."

He replied, "I will print fifty for you for free." It was good I was able to go with my mom, and I was thankful to speak up about her needs.

Next he wanted to know what message to put on the gravestone. There was room for twenty-two characters, so we took the paper to think and pray about it.

When we first arrived at the funeral home, the director placed a call to schedule a date for the service. "We are on hold and twenty-eighth in line," he said. Later, when he asked for the army discharge paper, my mom gave him what she had. "That is not the right paper. Do you have the correct paper?"

"I think so," she replied. We had to hurry home and return by five with the right one. We returned with the correct document, but the delay meant they would need to call the scheduler the next day and call us back. This turned out to be providential because by the time they got through to the scheduler the next day, the service had to be delayed another week. This gave us more time for planning and also for our relatives to make plans to come.

After much consideration and prayer, we settled on "Safe in God's hands" for Dad's headstone. What a precious promise!

You will rise to receive your allotted inheritance

Almost a year after my dad died, Mom and I wanted to see the gravestone we had chosen. We decided to visit on Memorial Day because the military cemetery places flags on every grave, and we stood in awe of the sight of myriads of flags. I'm sure we will be reunited with Dad in heaven someday, and there are so many promises that encourage me, such as 1 Corinthians 15:23, "But each in turn: Christ, the firstfruits; then, when he comes, those who belong to him." Just like my dad rests, so Daniel was also told he would rest and wait. Daniel 12:13 shares,

Prayer Still Moves Mountains

"As for you, go your way till the end. You will rest, and then at the end of the days you will rise to receive your allotted inheritance."

What startled me that Memorial Day was the sheer number of people. When I began to look around, I noticed many huddled by grave sites. Just a row behind us there was a woman holding a younger man. I walked over and mentioned our loss and asked about hers. We hugged, and then shared our hope in Jesus. Next, I noticed a woman sitting beside a grave a few rows away. She had spread a blanket on the grass and had journals and food. When I got close, she reached up to hug me as I reached down to hug her. She was there to remember her husband. Mom and I came away really impressed that this was a place of ministry.

The next year, I wanted to see if I could encourage anyone else. Driving down one hill I gasped to see really small graves on a hillside. Out of curiosity I pulled over, jumped out, walked closer. I saw a woman tucked back in the woods sitting on a rock. Strolling closer, I asked, "Do you need a hug?"

She replied, "My husband died ten years ago, yet it is all still so fresh."

We hugged, and I encouraged and wished her well. These encounters reminded me that it's important to reach out and listen to people's stories, so they don't continue suffering alone.

Jesus lasts

When Jesus was on earth, He stepped out of the wilderness and into ministry. He reached out to people again and again. He blessed little children. He made friends with women. You know the stories:

- Jesus reached out to Nicodemus.
- Jesus reached out to the Samaritan woman.
- Jesus reached out to the first disciples.
- Jesus reached out to Matthew.
- Jesus reached out to the rich young man.
- Jesus reached out to a demon-possessed man.
- Jesus reached out to the woman caught in adultery.

Something That Lasts

- Jesus reached out to Zacchaeus.

Jesus dined with tax collectors and sinners, and He pointed them to the one thing that lasts—His kingdom.

People felt as though they could call on Jesus for anything. One day Jesus received word that one of His friends, Lazarus, was very sick. John 11:3 states, "So the sisters sent word to Jesus, 'Lord, the one you love is sick.' " Continuing on, we read that Jesus loved Martha and her sister and Lazarus, yet when He heard that Lazarus was sick, He stayed where He was two more days (verses 5, 6).

As time went by, Martha and Mary had to start wondering. Perhaps they started to think of reasons for His delay as Lazarus steadily grew worse. Perhaps they remembered the last time Jesus was eating in their home. I imagine He may have looked across the table and said, "Martha, I just appreciate your hospitality so much. Your food is exceptional, and your friendship always warms My heart. If there is ever anything you need, Martha, just let Me know. You can call me anytime." But then the unthinkable happened. Jesus didn't arrive, Lazarus died, and they had to bury him. They wrapped Lazarus in cloths, put him in the tomb, and rolled the stone across the entrance.

Did the sisters remember Job's words, "I know that my redeemer lives, and that in the end he will stand upon the earth. And after my skin has been destroyed, yet in my flesh I will see God; I myself will see him with my own eyes—I, and not another. How my heart yearns within me!" (Job 19:25–27)?

They didn't ponder long, because suddenly Jesus appeared on the scene. Martha asked her burning question, "Lord, if you had been here, my brother would not have died. But I know that even now God will give you whatever you ask" (John 11:21, 22). *Jesus, where were You when I needed You?*

That day, Jesus did the impossible: He raised Lazarus to life. His compassion and love for the sisters reinforced and multiplied. And His power over death was a staggering proof of His divinity. Now, we await the day when He will do that for our loved ones. Revelation 2:7

Prayer Still Moves Mountains

shares, "To the one who is victorious, I will give the right to eat from the tree of life, which is in the paradise of God." And I believe that day will be soon!

We do have something that lasts. It is the same covenant Jesus made with Adam and Eve, Abraham, and Moses. He came to earth to carry it out, and now we share the same hope of a risen Lord—this same Jesus will come again! So I urge you to choose Jesus. His covenant of love is the only thing that lasts. He is reaching out to us—offering something that lasts.

Reflection

1. Are you comfortable talking with people about death? If not, do you want to seek out a pastor or elder in your church to discuss how to be more comfortable?

2. Look up verses on death and journal your thoughts.

3. Are you encouraged that we have something that lasts? Please find someone to share this with.

Chapter 14

Forward With Urgency

And do this, understanding the present time: The hour has already come for you to wake up from your slumber, because our salvation is nearer now than when we first believed.
—Romans 13:11

I find it hard to eat my breakfast if I see the birds at the feeder outside the kitchen window are out of food. Setting my breakfast down, I grab the shelled sunflower seeds and go outside to fill the feeder. I've discovered that shelled sunflower seeds seem to attract the most birds, especially the lovely yellow goldfinches. Similarly, I find it hard to go about life when others are hungering for the things of God. There is not much time left before Jesus comes. To me, keeping the eternal in focus is helpful, and praying to be in the right place at the right time often leads to amazing encounters. I know that our work for the Lord matters, and small tasks build up and connect God's kingdom piece by piece. We will reap joy and peace now and eternal rewards later if we stay focused. I often find myself praying, "Lord, please open my eyes to the mission opportunities in front of me."

As I write this chapter, my mom is in the hospital with intestinal challenges and I am sitting in her room. The day before, she came by ambulance and was suffering intense pain. The emergency-room team did a number of tests, and she finally had some relief after receiving pain medication. While waiting for Mom to be seen, I dashed out to my car to bring in a few of her things. As I walked out, one of my

Prayer Still Moves Mountains

friends entered with her husband, who was bleeding from a severe leg wound. When I got outside, I called another friend to pray with me for them. How I long for the day when suffering and pain will end!

To me, *moving forward with urgency* is being focused on doing what I can—what God is putting in front of me. Even sitting in my mom's hospital room, I can pray for the gunshot victim in the next room and the police officers outside his room. Today, as I passed by the waiting room and saw the board listing all the people in operations, I offered a prayer for them too. It's always good to stop and pray as we go through our day. When a man from admitting came in with a paper for me to sign for my mom, I sent up a silent prayer for him as he left the room. In fact, so many people came to my mom's room it felt like Grand Central Station! The busyness reminds me of the mission of *moving forward with urgency* because everyone needs to hear about Jesus.

A storm is coming

In Mark 4, Jesus was in a boat sharing the parable of a farmer going out to sow his seed. Later, when alone with His disciples, Jesus was asked what the parable meant. He responded, "The farmer sows the word. Some people are like seed along the path, where the word is sown. As soon as they hear it, Satan comes and takes away the word that was sown in them. Others, like seed sown on rocky places, hear the word and at once receive it with joy. But since they have no root, they last only a short time. When trouble or persecution comes because of the word, they quickly fall away" (verses 14–17).

Jesus' story reminds me of how we need to know the storm is coming in advance and have a plan for how we will hold on to truth. We know that if the seed that falls to the ground doesn't take root, it will be blown by the wind. Meanwhile, a "storm" is coming, world events are rather chaotic, but when the chaos surrounds us, "God moments" shine through to remind us that He is with us. God will respond when we reach out to Him for help. Some people store up food and supplies. Some people are not interested in reading Daniel and Revelation in advance or asking God for help. As the storm on our horizon grows,

Forward With Urgency

there will be wars and rumors of wars. While earthly wars may happen, ultimately the war described in Revelation is more a battle for control of your mind and actions. Revelation 12:17 states, "Then the dragon was enraged at the woman and went off to wage war against the rest of her offspring—those who keep God's commands and hold fast their testimony about Jesus." Let's prepare by studying prophecy, remembering God's comforting promises, and focus on reaching out to others with God's love. Jesus will come soon!

Reaching out from the "Garden of Prayer"

There is a lovely "Garden of Prayer" area at the Gladstone Campground—where many believers gather for the Oregon Conference Camp Meeting. It usually has a tent to provide shelter from the sun where people may sit, read, and pray. Nearby, but also in the garden, is another gazebo area with seats that overlook the beautiful flowers and greenery. A team of volunteers monitor the prayer garden during camp meeting, and I enjoy volunteering there. During my shift at the prayer garden, I pray that God will help me connect with the right people, and I am delighted with each opportunity to connect with the people who come by.

I find it encouraging to meet people at the Garden of Prayer and watch some answers to prayer happen. A few examples include one woman who found the housing she needed and another who received a job offer. Every day at 5:30 p.m. prayer staff meet to pray over cards collected from various drop sites throughout the grounds where people place prayer requests. The organizers of the meetings for children ages five and six had made prayer cards for them to fill in. These were sent to the prayer team as well—these requests were so cute and heartfelt.

Another time, I met a child as she was exiting the garden area. She was holding a stuffed rabbit, and I commented, "Hey, that is a really cute rabbit."

She replied back, "This rabbit is supposed to remind me to pray to God."

"That's great," I responded. Then I thought to myself, *Wow, someone*

Prayer Still Moves Mountains

is really doing a great job with these kids.

One day I remembered something else I wanted at the bookstore and walked over to the nearby Adventist Book Center. While looking at the gluten-free food a woman that had helped me on a previous visit approached me. I shared that the Garden of Prayer team was praying for the bookstore.

She replied, "Thank you. It could use prayer. I also have a personal request," and she proceeded to share her story. We prayed together right then, and I thought, *This was another providential connection.* It is fulfilling to be in the right place at the right time!

A few days later on Friday, Corleen, Linda and I were in the cafeteria at the camp grounds, and Corleen mentioned, "We don't have anyone to pray with people in the Garden of Prayer Sabbath afternoon. Would you and Linda consider being there?"

"Maybe we could be there from two to three. What do you think, Linda?" I replied.

"That would probably work for me," Linda said.

The next day I arrived at two o'clock at the prayer tent and sat down. After a few minutes, I prayed, "Heavenly Father, I can occupy this place for the time I said I would, and it may be a quiet hour, but I also know You can make a connection happen."

Moments later, a man walked up and asked, "Is this a good place for quiet prayer?"

"Yes, and there are a few books and pamphlets on the table if you would like to read," I affirmed.

He stepped into the tent with me and took a chair. I couldn't help wondering what would happen when Linda arrived because I couldn't picture her being quiet for long. She has an enthusiastic personality and a lot to say. However, I didn't feel compelled to let the man know that someone else would be coming. I just waited to see what would happen. The man reached for a book and started to leaf through it.

A few minutes went by, and then Linda walked up and sat down in the chair by the door. First, she looked at me. Then she looked at the man and then back at me, and I recognized that she could hardly contain her excitement. Sure enough, she soon eagerly shared, "You'll never guess who I ran into on my way here! As I was on my way, I noticed that Dr. Bertlinski was right next to my tent, and I stopped and spoke with him."

"Wow," I said, "that's amazing!" I remembered that he had spoken at a health fair that I'd helped Linda's church host.

She continued to share about their visit when the man who had arrived earlier piped up, "I know Dr. Bertlinski from Loma Linda. He was two years behind me in school. Do you think he is still there? I would really like to see him."

"He probably is. He's just down the hill and to the right, near the tents," she confirmed.

Then I chimed in, "Linda, this seems important, would you take this man to the exact place so he can connect with Dr. Bertlinski?" And off they went.

As I reflected about yet another connection that God arranged, it occurred to me that it's as simple as making ourselves available and praying for God to make connections happen. He knows who to connect and how. What a blessing it is when we meet people and share Jesus with them!

Peter focused on Jesus Christ
In Acts 3, Peter and John were on their way to the temple to pray. A lame man that begged at the gate named Beautiful arrested their attention with a plea for money. Acts records, "Then Peter said, 'Look at us!' So the man gave them his attention, expecting to get something from them. Then Peter said, 'Silver or gold I do not have, but what I do have I give you. In the name of Jesus Christ of Nazareth, walk.' Taking him by the right hand, he helped him up, and instantly the man's feet and ankles became strong" (verses 4–7). A crowd gathered, and Peter took the opportunity to share important details—who killed Jesus and why, and the good news that they could repent and turn to God. I like the part where he gives credit to Jesus for healing the man, "By faith in the name of Jesus, this man whom you see and know was

made strong. It is Jesus' name and the faith that comes through him that has completely healed him, as you can all see" (verse 16).

Near the end of Peter's life, he wrote some advice to church leaders. During that time churches in other provinces were being persecuted, and he wanted to encourage the believers to remain faithful. The book of 1 Peter can be briefly outlined:

- First, he urges believers to be holy in everything they do (1 Peter 1:15).
- Second, he explains that godly living will impress those who might accuse and persecute without just cause (1 Peter 3:13–16).
- Third, he acknowledges that they may suffer for their faith, but it is to be expected. After all, Jesus suffered. And he encouraged them to wait for the day when Jesus will return (1 Peter 4, 5).

In the same way, we too should strive to live holy lives, let the Holy Spirit make us more like Jesus, and take courage when we face persecution and suffering.

Jesus cares

Charles Spurgeon, the great nineteenth-century London preacher, recognized that people are worried about many things, and he shared this observation,

> A little London girl, who had gone into the country, once said, "Look, mamma, at that poor little bird; it has not got any cage!" That would not have struck me as a being any loss to the bird; and if you and I were without our cage, and the box of seed, and glass of water, it would not be much of a loss if we were cast adrift into the glorious liberty of a life of humble dependence upon God. It is that cage of carnal trust, and that box of seed that we are always laboring to fill, that

makes the worry of this mortal life; but he who has grace to spread his wings and soar away, and get into the open field of divine trustfulness, may sing all the day.[1]

This reminds me of helping the Community Services program at the Gladstone Park church. Every Thursday, for several months, during the COVID-19 pandemic we received USDA food boxes to give out. The boxes come chilled with various meats, dairy, vegetables, and fruits all in one convenient box. Then the boxes have to immediately be dispersed to prevent spoilage. Thankfully, we had several volunteers who would show up and deliver boxes to various locations.

Abraham is an example of someone who followed God's instructions, because of who God is. Charles Spurgeon made this observation about Abraham, "The faith of Abraham could lead strings of camels and flocks of sheep away from Haran to Canaan. His was the faith which could drive the tent-pin into a foreign soil, or roll up the canvas. It is a practical, active, living, week-day, every-day faith. . . . We need a bread and cheese faith, . . . a faith which believes that God who feeds the ravens will send us our daily bread."[2]

Jesus promises us in Matthew 6:26, "Look at the birds of the air; they do not sow or reap or store away in barns, and yet your heavenly Father feeds them. Are you not much more valuable than they?" Jesus cares about us, and He will supply all that we need. Daily, He invites us to rest in this knowledge.

Reaching out in Juneau, Alaska

People down through the ages have used a huge variety of ministry opportunities for sharing Jesus with others. People sometimes think that the word *ministry* is vague; however, I think ministry is simply something we do for the Lord. Colossians 3:23, 24 asserts, "Whatever you do, work at it with all your heart, as working for the Lord, not for human masters, since you know that you will receive an inheritance from the Lord as a reward. It is the Lord you are serving."

It was May 13, 2016, and I had been invited to share at a women's

Prayer Still Moves Mountains

retreat in Juneau, Alaska. When I sat down in the Portland terminal waiting to board, I checked the boarding time for my flight and noticed it was past time. *Oh no, did I miss it?* I wondered as I jumped up to ask a gate agent.

"No, your flight is delayed forty minutes," she said. There were hundreds of people milling in the area, and it was loud because there were five gates in close proximity. I turned to my left and saw an older man a few feet from me holding his driver's license and boarding pass. I said, "You can put away your license. You only have to show your boarding pass."

"What?" he replied.

I repeated myself.

"OK" he said. "I have a hard time hearing and haven't heard any of the announcements."

"What's your flight number?" I asked.

"2570," he replied.

"They are boarding right now, all rows, over there," I said and pointed to another gate.

"They are?" he asked.

"Yes," I replied as he went to board. I thought, *If I hadn't said something, he might have missed his flight because he hadn't heard the necessary information.*

I had a lovely time with the ladies in Alaska. It always feels similar to a family reunion when I spend time with like-minded, mission-oriented believers. We stayed in a small house with two levels and had a blessed time sharing, studying the Bible, and praying together.

When I arrived, Lynne, one of the weekend organizers, said to me, "You came during the best weather we have. The forecast calls for three seventy-degree days."

The retreat was located eighteen miles outside of Juneau, near the ocean, and had a refreshing atmosphere.

"How's this for a retreat?" they asked me.

"Beautiful," I replied.

Then they counseled, "Please watch for bears, and don't hike alone."

Forward With Urgency

Sabbath afternoon we relaxed in the sun by the water. Then on Sunday, Lynne and Nickie took me to breakfast before Lynne drove me the rest of the way to the airport. We prayed together and asked that God would bless my flight to Portland and also the ministry team and opportunities in Juneau. As my flight took off, I thought about the faith-filled and refreshing time I'd had on the retreat. How I look forward to heaven, which I imagine may feel like a never-ending retreat, so many opportunities to reach out and connect with fellow believers to anticipate!

Wrong seat is the right seat

In the Juneau terminal, as I waited to leave for Portland, I checked my boarding pass and saw that my seat was 8A. Later, when I boarded the airplane, I watched the numbers above the seats and located it. A man was sitting on the aisle, and a little girl was in the middle. I commented, "I'm the window seat beside you guys."

The man jumped up and said, "I'll help you with your luggage as soon as I help this lady." I didn't object—I'm always thankful when someone offers to help. I moved to the window and sat down. I usually try to say something to my seatmates, so I asked the man after he sat down, "Do you live in Seattle?"

He replied, "No, we live in Juneau."

Then our conversation was halted because the stewardess stopped by our seats and looked at me. "What seat number are you?" she asked.

"I'm 8A."

"Are you sure you are not 9A?"

"I'm 8A," I replied.

"Seat 8A is one row in front of you," she said and turned to a man in front of her. "She is sitting in your seat. Do you want to just sit one row ahead in 8A?"

"That's fine," he said. He squeezed in in front of me, turned to a woman he passed over and said, "Gloria, is that you? I can't believe you're here." I tuned out then tuned back in when he picked up his phone and called someone. Then I heard, "Can you believe I'm sitting

Prayer Still Moves Mountains

by Gloria? Guess where Gloria is going. She's going to San Francisco."

Wow, I thought, *my being in the wrong seat resulted in this man sitting by someone he needed to see.*

The man in my row turned to me and asked, "What were you doing in Juneau?"

"I was sharing at a women's retreat," I replied.

"What church did you do that for?" he asked.

I shared, and then his daughter who sat between us got excited and said, "I'm going to a Bible camp this summer!" She told me all about it.

As I listened to her enthusiastic description, I thought, *I sat in the wrong seat that turned out to be the right seat for me and for the man now sitting in front of me.*

How precious it was to find a child hungering for the things of God! Moving forward with urgency is being focused on doing what I can—whatever God puts in front of me, whether it's a small task or a large project.

Reflection

1. What do you do when you notice people are hungry for the Word of God?

2. Read all the stories in Mark 4 and find a friend to share what you are doing to prepare for "storms" that come.

3. Have you ever been in the wrong place that turned out to be the right place?

4. Journal a story of a time you reached out to someone for prayer. Or please pray for the opportunity to pray with someone.

Forward With Urgency

1. Charles Spurgeon, "Prayer, the Cure for Care," *The Spurgeon Center*, accessed April 5, 2022, https://www.spurgeon.org/resource-library/sermons/prayer-the-cure-for-care/#flipbook/.

2. *The Promise, Adult Sabbath School Bible Study Guide*, Teacher's Edition, no. 504, (April–June 2021), 159.

Chapter 15

Called to Pray

Jabez cried out to the God of Israel, "Oh, that you would bless me and enlarge my territory! Let your hand be with me, and keep me from harm so that I will be free from pain." And God granted his request.
—1 Chronicles 4:10

I find the simplicity of Jabez's story reassuring—Jabez prayed and God granted his request. One day, as I thought about the plea, "Oh Lord bless me indeed and enlarge my territory," the Holy Spirit began reminding me of other examples. One was how Elisha said that he wanted a double portion of Elijah's spirit. In 2 Kings 2:9 it shares,

> When they had crossed, Elijah said to Elisha, "Tell me, what can I do for you before I am taken from you?"
> "Let me inherit a double portion of your spirit," Elisha replied.

Another example was how the Canaanite woman pressed in with her need to Jesus in Matthew 15:28, "Then Jesus said to her, 'Woman, you have great faith! Your request is granted.' And her daughter was healed at that moment." These are amazing stories of people reaching out in faith and receiving the blessing.

It was January 1, 2013, and I felt compelled to pray for forty days at the beginning of the year that God would open the door for ministry.

Called to Pray

My request for 2013 was that it be full of interesting encounters and opportunities for soul winning—and that at the end of the year I would have a closer relationship with Jesus. For forty days I highlighted a few people and a specific topic to pray about. On January 8, I prayed specifically for my friend Bev.

My friend Bev grew up in a Christian home with an eager willingness to share about Jesus wherever she could. She especially has a talent for hospitality. She quickly notices those who seem in need of a friend and invites them for a meal. She also notices people who need various items and finds a way to help them. She often has Bible studies going with people who are searching for Jesus. Over the years, I've spent a lot of time with Bev and her husband, Wayne. We've often prayed, visited people in need, or helped with other mission-type projects together. She has preached in her local church and also in Africa. We have the "ready to go for Jesus" desire and perspective in common. It was quite natural that when I found a brochure with an invitation to Page, Arizona, I thought immediately of Bev.

I saw the brochure on an information desk while attending an Oregon Adventist Men's Chorus concert for an Adventist-laymen's Services and Industries meeting. Wondering what the brochure was advertising, I picked it up and saw that it showed people working in a mission setting and it peaked my interest. I had come to enjoy the music, and now it felt as though God was inviting me to participate in something more.

The front of the brochure said, "Diné Outreach Reaching the Navajo Nation for Jesus." Then, "Come be a missionary in the untouched western Navajo nation." And it shared a list of some things people could do. I looked around, but there was no one to answer any questions. Sensing that God might be calling me to look into this opportunity, I took the brochure with me.

Reaching out to people in Page

Monday morning, I phoned the number on the brochure and left a message. It was Thursday, May 9, when Kelley returned my call. I related, "Kelley, my name is Diane Pestes, and I found your brochure inviting people to come to Page. Were you at the ASI convention?"

"I was there on Friday for a brief time and placed the brochures on the information desk, but then we had to leave. I prayed over those brochures before I left and asked that God would lead someone to find them," she said.

"That really is amazing, because I felt compelled to look at this particular brochure. Do you still have a need for people to come? And what types of things do they do?" I asked.

"We have had a youth group work on the building, and there are a lot of needs with carpentry in our sanctuary space. Many electrical wires need to be replaced. We also have had people come that did some cooking classes," she replied.

"Well, I am not a builder. But I could ask around to see if I know anyone who'd be able to help. I could do some talks if you have a need for that."

"That would be great, Diane," Kelley replied.

We chatted some more, and she asked for my email address and phone number to send me more information. We talked about a possible weekend event, perhaps a prayer conference. And I made a few calls to ask about helping with the building, but I didn't find any takers. In another conversation with Kelley, she confirmed the prayer conference weekend would be a blessing for the church.

The one-minute missionary

"Hello Bev, how are you?" I asked her on the phone.

"I am doing great," she said.

"Bev, Ron and I went to the ASI convention recently, and when I was in the lobby I found a brochure with an invitation to Page, Arizona. I thought of you as someone who could help me. Would you be interested in going there with me to preach? We would lead a prayer conference over a weekend, and we could both share messages. Would you be interested?"

"Let me think about it and ask Wayne. Maybe we could fly there," she suggested.

On June 22, Bev texted that she was willing to go to Page with me, and she confirmed that Wayne could fly us there. "As long as we can

Called to Pray

find a weekend that works," she continued. "Wayne says it will take four and a half hours to fly there."

A few more phone calls with Kelley, and we figured out that September 27–29 was a weekend that worked for everyone and we began planning in earnest. It worked out that we'd have five presentations from Friday night through Sunday morning. Bev and I would take turns sharing about the theme "Prayer Works."

As we finalized our plans, Bev and I were eager to include our prayer partners, who were excited to receive updates and pray for our upcoming trip. Our first update included some general information about the town and the local Adventist church, as well as a list of prayer requests:

- God's message of love to change lives
- God's blessing on all involved (and the community)
- God's mighty Holy Spirit power for everything
- Safety and health
- Good flying weather
- Advertising effectiveness
- Visitations—that we would find many residents desiring prayer

Moving forward in prayer

In life, we pray and move forward as God opens doors. When obstacles come, we pray and continue to move forward as God guides us. Knowing this, I wasn't too surprised when Bev phoned me on the evening of September 24 to say that "the weather for Thursday doesn't look good for flying, and it looks better Friday, but it might be a bumpy ride."

I responded, "Well thankfully it will still get us there in time for Friday night's meeting. Lord, may Your will be done." And I made haste to write a second update to our prayer partners.

> Dear Prayer Partners,
>
> Due to some icy conditions in Madras on Thursday, we will now be flying out Friday morning. We still hope to come back on Sunday. However, the weather for Sunday

doesn't look good and Monday isn't ideal. Thank you for your prayers for the weather.

We are claiming Psalm 139:9, 10, "If I rise on the wings of the dawn, if I settle on the far side of the sea, even there your hand will guide me, your right hand will hold me fast."

Lois's husband, Dave, pointed out to me that even though Arizona is in the Mountain Time Zone, their time is the same as ours. I had looked it up on the internet, and it looked different in Page than in Tucson. Thus today I had an interesting conversation with the Chamber of Commerce lady. She said, "God set the time and we go by His time and don't ever change like the rest of the country." Now you can figure the times to pray for the meetings.

Prayer works, Diane, Bev, and Wayne

Adapting as the adventure begins

Friday, September 27, we got up very early, ate a small breakfast, and then headed to the airport. Wayne thought it would take four and a half hours to reach Page, and soon we landed safely in Arizona.

No one was there to meet us in Page as we pulled up in our rental car Friday mid-morning. When we reached the church, we walked around the church building and discovered a trailer on the side and knocked on the door. Several minutes later, a man named Kent answered our knock, and he had a key to the church. He proved very helpful by showing us around and helping run the sound system. To save funds, I had asked Kelley if I could stay at the church in one of the rooms. I assumed that I would be alone in the church, so I was very surprised when we arrived and found out that three rooms were already occupied by people who needed a place to live!

After a while, Bev, Wayne and I became very hungry and left to eat lunch at a Mexican restaurant before returning to prepare for the evening meeting. Meanwhile, Wayne had been monitoring the forecast closely, and he told us, "A major storm is coming Saturday afternoon for several days, and I will need to fly the plane out tomorrow. I may not be able to come back for you."

Called to Pray

Bev and I exchanged a glance—what an opportunity to adapt to any and all circumstances!

That afternoon I emailed a message to our prayer partners:

> Dear Prayer Partners,
>
> We arrived in Page after a lovely flight. The scenic red rocks between St. George, Utah, and Page, Arizona, were especially beautiful. Here in Page we are enjoying blue sky and high sixties. We have been to the church and met some wonderful people, and we look forward to our first meeting this evening. I can describe the words "mission trip" in this way: God is in charge, and we can always expect minute by minute changes. Tomorrow Bev and I will watch as Wayne leaves with the plane due to worsening weather in Madras (potentially lasting through Thursday). The Avis rental company here told us we couldn't take their car back to Oregon. We think someone here will drive us back to St. George (two hours west of Page), where there is an international airport and we will see about renting a car there. Please pray that we know God's will—He knows best. Also, my friend Linda's daughter needs prayer. She is in the emergency room.
>
> Prayer works—thanks, Diane, Bev, and Wayne

Blessed by tea and stories

Our evening meeting went very well, and after chatting with those attending and praying with a few, Bev and Wayne went to their hotel and I walked upstairs to my room. Since it was too early for me to sleep, I wandered down the hall to see if I could talk with Lisa. She was in the kitchen and made some tea for us. "Diane, I really enjoyed your talk and the practical applications. I like how you shared about being grateful and thankful while you walk and pray because it makes the devil flee. Also, I appreciate your suggestion about praying through the alphabet using God's attributes—I think of Almighty, Beloved and Creator, and so on."

"Thanks, Lisa. I appreciate that. It is so good to finally be here and

Prayer Still Moves Mountains

now to meet you—and have a new friend. Could you share some stories about your experience here?"

Lisa began, "My husband, Dale, has been sanding the drywall around the whole church building. He gets down on his hands and knees to sweep up the shavings with a little broom because the bigger broom broke and there are no funds to replace it. One day he was on a ladder at the front of the church trying to remove a speaker. When suddenly the speaker flipped over catching him off guard, and he lost his balance and fell on his head. His angel must have cushioned the fall because he was unhurt and got right back up and started working again!"

She continued, "There are days we go out to the Navajo reservation and help with various needs. One time a dental clinic was held, and people came very early and from long distances. Since it was cold with snow on the ground, we served hot beverages while they waited. I needed to go into town for supplies and went out to start my car but it wouldn't start. I tried several times, but it just wouldn't start. I went back in and decided to wait an hour and try again. I tried three times, waiting an hour between each try, with no results. Before I could try a fourth time, I met a lady who had come for the clinic and had also requested prayer. We prayed together for at least a half hour. After our prayer time, I went outside to try my car and it started right up. As I thought about it later, I figured that if the car had started earlier I would have missed the opportunity to pray with that lady. What a blessing!"

Sabbath "God moments"

Sabbath evening, I sent out another update:

> Dear Prayer Partners,
>
> Thank you for praying. We are having special "God moments" left and right! Here are a few examples:
>
> - Avis phoned today and told us that we could trade in our current rental car on Sunday for one we could drive to Redmond, Oregon.

Called to Pray

- Linda's daughter is out of the ER and doing much better.
- During Sabbath School, a distraught lady came rushing to the front stating that a dog had been hit by a car outside, broke its foot, was limping, and someone needed to take it to the vet. Seth, the Bible Worker, said he would go look. Immediately I said a prayer for help and followed Seth outside. Rounding the corner, I saw the lady saying, "I don't know what happened. I don't know what happened. He's fine now." That was a quick answer to my prayer!

God is good—we have two more meetings here followed by our trip home, and we are seeing changed lives and praying as the Holy Spirit leads us.

Thank you for your continued prayers, Diane and Bev

Siri knows some; God knows all

Bev had gone on a drive with a group, and they were late getting back to the church. They might have been much later if it hadn't been for Siri, Apple's virtual assistant, who seems to know right where you are—most of the time. As dusk approached, they took a wrong turn and were not sure which road to take back. Bev asked Siri for help, and Siri led them turn by turn, back to the church. When they arrived, we gathered for a meeting. It was Bev's turn, and her topic was "When God Is Silent."

She shared, "Since we are running a bit late, I'll make this shorter. I am thankful God knows where we are at all times! We had a nice time viewing beautiful scenery but missed a turn on our way back, and Siri had to help us with directions.

"Sometimes it seems as though God is silent. The Bible tells about miracles that happened instantaneously—like when fire fell in answer to Elijah's prayer on Mount Carmel and when Jesus raised Jairus's daughter and Lazarus from the dead. However, sometimes God waits for better timing. There are many wonderful examples of this in the Bible too, like the delay of Sarah and Abraham having a baby. God's timing was perfect, and Genesis 21:1 explains how God came through, 'Now the Lord was

Prayer Still Moves Mountains

gracious to Sarah as he had said, and the LORD did for Sarah what he had promised.' I also think sometimes God uses people with extra faith to show that it is better to wait for God's timing to receive answers to prayer.

"I remember when my husband and I were on a mission trip to Zimbabwe two years ago. We visited a church and school campus that had opened a few months before. We were told of a woman there who had some property that she gave to the Lord. It was many acres, and she wanted to have a church and school on the land. She had gone every day to the property and knelt and prayed that God would make it possible to have a Christian school there, so the little children of her town could learn about Him. Every day for twenty-one years she went to this property and prayed. Finally, Maranatha heard the story and a team came and built a large school campus with a beautiful church. As a result, many people in that town were able to send their children to learn of the God who answered her prayer. Her twenty-one-year-old prayer had gone on so long many people knew about it. She never gave up in her faith that God would answer her prayer in His timing. God seemed silent for so many years, but she had faith and did not give up. I wonder if I have that kind of faith?"

All too soon it was time for our last meeting on Sunday morning. I was especially thankful for the reminder that God knows everything, because after the meeting Bev and I would be leaving to drive back to Oregon. We would trust God to go in front of us and clear the heavy rain that was predicted. Wayne had let us know that he had encountered seventy-five-mile-per-hour winds during his return flight, and the turbulence had caused him to hit his head on the ceiling once! He told us, "You would not have enjoyed flying!"

It's all about Jesus

I firmly believe that the most important blessing we have is Jesus, so I started Sunday's talk with a brief recap and testimony transition to the need for Jesus. When I was very young, my parents kept talking with me about how someday I would need a huge operation—open heart surgery. They walked me through little rituals: pretending to check me in at the hospital, pretending to take my temperature, and pretending

Called to Pray

to be in the recovery room. They talked about everything that would happen with the intention that when I got to the real thing I wouldn't be scared. In a similar way, I have observed God do something like that.

After Adam and Eve sinned, God introduced the concept of offering a lamb as a sacrifice for their sins, which was intended to point to Jesus, the Lamb of God who takes away the sins of the world (John 1:29). Because of Jesus' sacrifice, our sins can be forgiven and we can live a life of service to our Savior. When we choose to follow Him, God writes His law on our hearts. In 2 Corinthians 3:3, Paul wrote, "You show that you are a letter from Christ, the result of our ministry, written not with ink but with the Spirit of the living God, not on tablets of stone but on tablets of human hearts." As the psalmist says, keeping God's law becomes a delight, "I delight to do thy will, O my God: yea, thy law is within my heart" (Psalm 40:8, KJV). If God's authority is a delight to follow, it will help us demolish the strongholds of sin.

One key way to think about how to do this is to focus on what Jesus thought about. We can have true healing for the mind by focusing on what Jesus' mind thought about. Second Timothy 1:7 shares, "For God hath not given us the spirit of fear; but of power, and of love, and of a sound mind" (KJV). And Philippians 2:5 shares, "Let this mind be in you, which was also in Christ Jesus" (KJV).

How did Jesus have a sound mind? What did Jesus think about? Think of it in these five examples:

1. He thought about other people's needs.
2. He thought about His Father's will.
3. He always talked about the kingdom of heaven, and not His own will.
4. He was constantly emptied of self. He had no agenda of His own other than what His Father thought He should do each day.
5. He was empowered by the Holy Spirit.

Romans 8:26 shares, "In the same way, the Spirit helps us in our weakness." In Gethsemane, Jesus would have faltered if He hadn't surrendered to His Father's will. He prayed, "My Father, if it is possible, may this cup be taken from me. Yet not as I will, but as you will"

Prayer Still Moves Mountains

(Matthew 26:39). We all have moments when we want to give up, but that's exactly when we need to pray, claim Bible promises, and ask others to pray for us. Jesus fought His struggle through prayer. He asked His disciples to pray too, but sadly, they fell asleep and later their faith was shaken because they weren't prepared. It's important that we take time for prayer and Bible study in order to help us focus on Jesus.

After Bev and I hugged everyone goodbye and took pictures beside the church sign, we began our long drive home. That night we arrived in Salt Lake City, and then we were able to drive all the way to Madras the next day. What a blessing it was to be able to minister in Page, Arizona! I am so thankful for such friends as Bev, who want to serve wherever God opens a door. And I am grateful for our prayer partners who lifted our requests to God and contributed to our mission by blessing us with prayer. Let's stay ready to answer the call to pray whenever it comes.

Reflection

1. Have you ever prayed for your "territory" to increase? Did you journal about your experience and growth during that experience? What are you asking God for and recording now?

2. What process do you go through when it feels as though God is calling you to help Him with a project?

3. Would you consider finding a prayer partner (or a prayer team) if you don't already have one? Perhaps your local church has a prayer ministry you could join.

4. Consider inviting someone to a meal or coffee/tea with the purpose of sharing stories with each other and ending with prayer. It is amazing what God can do through these encounters!

5. The most important blessing we have is Jesus. What are you thankful for that He is doing for you?

Chapter 16

Prayer Still Moves Mountains

The name of the Lord is a fortified tower;
the righteous run to it and are safe.
—Proverbs 18:10

Every day of our life is an opportunity to share about what God has done and is doing in our lives. Then, when we get to heaven, we can share with even more people—how wonderful it will be to hear the testimonies of the saved! I think of the verse, "Let the redeemed of the Lord tell their story" (Psalm 107:2). Meanwhile, as the world looks to itself for solutions, we trust that "the name of the Lord is a strong tower; the righteous runneth into it and are safe" (Proverbs 18:10, KJV). When we run to Him, we are safe.

How can I recognize when God is at work? A few examples come to mind:

- This world is spiraling down into chaos, but sharing Jesus with others fills my life with joy and peace.
- Trying to plan ahead for every possibility or organize every single detail is overwhelming, but I find that when I pray about plans and details ahead of time, God brings the pieces together.
- It's hard to see so many broken lives in this world, but what a blessing it is to pray for someone and watch as God picks up the pieces and redeems them in spite of the brokenness.

Prayer Still Moves Mountains

- Studying God's Word, and especially the prophecies in Daniel and Revelation, I am encouraged to see how God has brought, and continues to bring, His church through the darkness and into His light, preparing us for an eternity with Him.
- As I participate in sharing Jesus with others, I am reminded that the battle will soon be over, but the war is already won. Jesus will come for His people soon.

When I recognize God's work in this world, I am filled with gratitude and praise—and that makes me excited to share Jesus with even more people. I believe that living in "chaos" is where "God moments" shine brightly—God loves to get our attention and He can and will respond to our needs.

Removing inner demons in others

"Could I help you with something while I am there?" I asked Bev.

It was Tuesday, May 31, 2016, and I was in Madras for a teeth cleaning at Wayne and Bev's dental office. Since the Madras Adventist Church runs the Jefferson County Food Bank on Tuesdays, I asked Bev if I could help there after my appointment. They open at 1:30 P.M., but people start lining up more than an hour before. Earlier in the year, Bev had started opening the door an hour ahead to chat, pray, and show DVDs about Jesus with those who were waiting for the food bank to open. This also gave people access to the bathroom, drinking water, tables, and chairs.

That Tuesday, Bev and I arrived early and prayed together in the prayer room before opening the door for those waiting. Immediately, Bev started to chat with a woman and asked her, "Is this your sister?"

"No, she is my daughter, and her mother is fighting with inner demons," she replied, referring to herself in the third person.

Soon Bev went to the front of the room and asked, "Before we start, is there anyone who wants someone to pray with them?"

The same woman held up her hand.

Prayer Still Moves Mountains

Bev pointed to a room and continued, "Diane is available to pray with you in the prayer room."

When she reached the prayer room, I introduced myself and the woman, named Jaime, started to sniffle and sadly said, "My husband left me, and I'm afraid to be alone. I have two kids, and I don't want my husband back unless he is a changed man. Every night my dead father appears in a dream on the end of my bed to tell me things and it really scares me."

As I listened, I realized this sounded like a visit from a demon, so I said to her, "Jamie, I don't believe that God wants you to be scared. Let's pray that you have good dreams and not bad ones. And let's also pray that God either changes your husband and brings him back to you or that God will keep him away. God is with you, and He has a plan for your life. He knows what's best for you, and He will take care of you and your children."

After I prayed with her, I felt compelled to ask, "Do you have a Bible?"

"I used to, but it got lost when I moved."

I motioned to Bev and asked, "Bev, can you find a Bible for Jamie?"

She replied, "Yes, I'll go find one."

As Bev left, I leaned toward Jamie and encouraged, "When you get your Bible, read it before you go to sleep and first thing when you wake up in the morning."

"That might help. I'll try that," she replied.

After watching the Jesus DVD, Bev stood up, said a prayer, and then people left the room. We immediately began rearranging the room for interviews and paperwork about what kind of food each client needed in their food box. A moment later, Jamie stepped back into the room and asked me, "My daughter keeps losing her place in her book. Do you have a bookmark?"

I thought to myself, *This is Providential because I have a laminated bookmark with me in my computer bag, and the bookmark I have along lists Scripture verses on the state of the dead.* I grabbed it and said, "Here's a bookmark for you, Jamie." What an encouraging God moment—I

Prayer Still Moves Mountains

was able to connect with Jamie, and then God set up an additional opportunity to share further Bible references with her.

Let's ask God to arrange connections for us every day. And let us trust in the name of the Lord, who "is a fortified tower, the righteous run to it and are safe" (Proverbs 18:10). He will provide the opportunities and the tools. All He asks of us is that "whatever you do, work at it with all your heart, as working for the Lord, not for human masters, since you know that you will receive an inheritance from the Lord as a reward. It is the Lord Christ you are serving" (Colossians 3:23, 24).

God at work in Boomer's life

There are many odd and scary things happening in our world right now, and it would be easy to fall into despair. Yet I'm thankful for the reminder that God works in the big and the small areas of our lives—He cares about even the smallest detail. I've often thought to myself, *If God displays His care for our Boomer, how much more does He care for us and our future?*

One day, Ron took Boomer out the front door for a bathroom break and then came back in. I crossed paths with them as I walked toward the laundry room, but suddenly remembered I had a question for Ron. When I turned around, I noticed Boomer was biting at something on his leg. It struck me as strange, and I ran over to look closer and noticed a yellow jacket on his leg. "Ron, come help!" I hollered. "There's a yellow jacket on Boomer's leg." Ron swatted it off but had already taken his shoes off, so I stepped on it to kill it. We got to it in time, and Boomer walked away without a sting—and so did Ron and I! That incident was a special reminder of God's care for humans and our pets.

On July 27, 2021, Ron and I decided to go out for breakfast and then enjoy a nature walk afterward. When we arrived home, our dogs, Boomer and Peanut, were very excited to see us and wanted lots of attention. Peanut followed me into our closet, and I reached down to pet him. Then Boomer joined us, but knowing that sometimes Peanut feels cornered, I picked up Boomer and set him on the bed to pet him. When I got down to his level, I noticed that his right eye was closed and weeping.

Prayer Still Moves Mountains

I showed Ron, and we phoned our vet, who said, "We can't get you in until next month."

We told them that wouldn't work, so they suggested a few places, but no one had an opening. A few places mentioned going to the VCA animal hospital, so we gave them a call. After we answered a few questions, they recommended that we bring Boomer to the emergency facility, so I took Boomer. As I waited for Boomer to be seen, I was thankful I had grabbed a book before we left home. Six hours later, I left with eye drops for an ulcer in Boomer's eye and instructions for caring for it. Many days later, after little sleep, a vet bill over $800, prayers with friends, and another vet appointment, Boomer's eye was healed. I am thankful for the animals God sends into our lives, and I am blessed as I watch how He provides and cares for them too.

AC power adapter found and brought in time

"I need you to bring my AC power adapter to downtown Portland because they don't have one here. I grabbed one that was the wrong size. Hurry quick, or you won't make it before rush-hour traffic begins." I awoke from a sound sleep and struggled to figure out what Ron was saying. It was 6:21 A.M., and Ron had left for a video job at about five thirty. This is just a small example of maintaining calm in a chaotic world. I changed clothes, grabbed the adapter, and ran for my truck, all the while calculating the time this would take—potentially an hour there and an hour back. Then I would have about forty minutes to get ready before I needed to leave for an assisted-living center where I was scheduled to share a devotional. *That should be just enough time*, I thought. Sure enough, I made it to Ron's location before the rush-hour traffic began.

When I arrived home, I sat down for breakfast, and I sensed God asking me, "Are you going to read the Bible this morning?"

Oh my, I thought, *I usually have a nice relaxed time with the Lord to read and pray, but this morning has prevented that. Dear God, please send me something quickly!*

Grabbing my Bible, I felt compelled to open it to the Gospels and

Prayer Still Moves Mountains

found myself in Luke 8, the parable of the sower. Verse 1, "After this, Jesus traveled about from one town and village to another, proclaiming the good news of the kingdom of God." Skipping to verses 4–8, it says,

> While a large crowd was gathering and people were coming to Jesus from town after town, he told this parable: "A farmer went out to sow his seed. As he was scattering the seed, some fell along the path; it was trampled on, and the birds ate it up. Some fell on rocky ground, and when it came up, the plants withered because they had no moisture. Other seed fell among thorns, which grew up with it and choked the plants. Still other seed fell on good soil. It came up and yielded a crop, a hundred times more than was sown."

"Jesus traveled about from one town and village to another, proclaiming the good news of the kingdom of God." I thought, *Wow that's what I like to do—proclaim the good news*. Reading on, verses 11 and 15 seemed to jump out at me, "This is the meaning of the parable: The seed is the word of God;" and "the seed on good soil stands for those with a noble and good heart, who hear the word, retain it, and by persevering produce a crop." I'm so thankful that God helps our seed planting efforts to have an effect.

Later Corleen called me and asked, "How was your day? I've been praying for you."

"Well, that explains a lot! God turned a hectic morning into a blessing. Then I gave a devotional talk at an assisted-living home, and it is always a blessing to share about Jesus. Thank you for your prayers!" I replied.

Finding a little girl

August is a great time to be in eastern Oregon for a few days of recreation. A friend and I set out one morning to kayak on Hosmer Lake. A thunderstorm hit us, and we got very wet. We were thankful to return to our lodging and dry off before eating a late lunch. That afternoon,

Prayer Still Moves Mountains

even though it still looked like it might rain, we decided to take our bikes on a ride to Benham Falls. When we reached the beautiful rushing water cascading down, we stared at it from the viewpoint for a bit and then headed back up a zigzag trail on our bikes. Suddenly a woman quickly approached us and asked, "Have you seen a little girl?"

We responded that we hadn't.

The woman hardly heard me and rushed ahead down the trail, and the man behind her explained, "Our daughter is missing. She is nine years old and about this tall," holding up his hand.

My friend replied, "We're on bikes and we will help you look, but first I have to use the bathroom over there." I took off down the trail while uplifting Psalm 120:1 in prayer, "I call on the Lord in my distress, and he answers me." When I returned, I found out that my friend tried the bathroom door and it was locked, and as she stood outside waiting she heard singing. She asked, "Is there someone in there?"

A little voice replied, "Yes."

"What is your name?" my friend asked.

When the girl said the name of the missing girl, my friend began calling for her parents because they had moved on with their search and were no longer in sight. They returned and were happily reunited with their daughter. As we started back on our bikes, it began raining and we got all wet again. But thinking about it later, we realized that had we not been there, the parents probably would have continued down the trail and after the girl finished in the bathroom she wouldn't have known which way to go and definitely ended up lost. God guided us that day so we could be there to make a connection between a girl who didn't know she was lost and her worried parents.

Praying four times helps

Some people approach worship with an organized routine, other people prefer to have fun and be flexible, and another group wants to see results. Thankfully, God is willing and able to work through each of these ways.

I tend to be serious, and I expect God to give results—like "ask and

Prayer Still Moves Mountains

receive," and it seems to work. But I also relate to Him as my Friend who knows me and cares for me. I think of the verse, "You do not have because you do not ask God" (James 4:2). I do know sometimes prayer results take decades or remain unanswered until God's kingdom.

One time a friend called to request prayer about a serious matter, and I suggested we fast and pray on an upcoming day specifically for her request. Then I added, "When I fast for a day, I usually like to pray for at least an hour about the special issue as well as when God impresses me throughout the day. However, since we are so busy, let's pray on the phone together in fifteen-minute increments four times on Tuesday."

We chose themes for each time. You may have heard of the acronym ACTS, which stands for adoration, confession, thanksgiving, and supplication. We were specifically praying for her book that was being released soon. Here is a short example of our prayer times:

- *Adoration:* "Lord, we thank You for providing opportunities to share our stories in books. You are so amazing—we adore You! We praise You for making a way for us to prosper in kingdom living."
- *Confession:* "Lord, we confess that we are not worthy to even write about Your goodness. Please forgive our meager attempts, and make Your message clear to all who read this book."
- *Thanksgiving:* "Lord, we thank You for hearing our requests for the success of this book. We claim Philippians 4:6, 7, realizing that we don't have to be anxious about anything, 'but in every situation, by prayer and petition, with thanksgiving, [we] present [our] requests to [You]. And the peace of God, which transcends all understanding, will guard [our] hearts and [our] minds in Christ Jesus.' "
- *Supplication:* "Lord, we ask that You would send this book into many homes and bless all who read it. We claim Ephesians 6:18, that shares we can pray 'in the Spirit on

Prayer Still Moves Mountains

all occasions with all kinds of prayers and requests. With this in mind, be alert and always keep on praying for all the Lord's people.' "

We prayed sentence prayers back and forth, claimed promises, and also read some passages that went along with the themes. Our plan to spread our prayer time over the course of a day provided space for further thought, and we would think of more things to pray over during our next prayer time. We had a special time, and the book did sell well.

One passage I love to pray through using ACTS is Isaiah's call to prophetic ministry. Isaiah didn't set out to be a prophet, but God commissioned him to be a messenger to people who thought they had God's favor but instead were disobedient. God gave Isaiah an unforgettable vision of His immenseness, power, and mystery.

Isaiah 6:1–3 shares, "In the year that King Uzziah died, I saw the Lord, high and exalted, seated on a throne; and the train of his robe filled the temple. Above him were seraphim, each with six wings: With two wings they covered their faces, with two they covered their feet, and with two they were flying. And they were calling to one another: 'Holy, holy, holy is the Lord Almighty; the whole earth is full of his glory.' "

- *Adoration:* This impressive scene causes us to be in awe of God. And an example prayer can start off with, "Lord, we adore You because You are holy, holy, holy."

- *Confession*: After Isaiah is moved with adoration he realizes his sinfulness in comparison. Isaiah records his confession in verses 4 and 5, "At the sound of their voices the doorposts and thresholds shook and the temple was filled with smoke. 'Woe to me!' I cried. 'I am ruined! For I am a man of unclean lips, and I live among a people of unclean lips, and my eyes have seen the King, the Lord Almighty.' " We might pray something along the lines of, "Heavenly Father, You know my life, please remove the sins You see in me, forgive me, and throw the sins into the deepest sea." God is instant with His response to Isaiah, and shares in verses 6 and 7, "Then one of the seraphim flew to me with a live coal in his hand, which he had taken with tongs from the altar. With it he touched my mouth and said, 'See, this has touched your lips; your guilt is taken away and your sin atoned for.' " A good cross reference verse for forgiveness is 1 John 1:9, "If we confess our sins, he is faithful and just and will forgive us our sins and purify us from all unrighteousness."

- *Thanksgiving:* God assured Isaiah, "Your guilt is taken away and your sin atoned for" (Isaiah 6:7). That's something to be thankful for! Isaiah doesn't seem to have time to express thanks here because things are happening so fast, but he was undoubtedly thankful. As we reflect on Isaiah's experience, we, too, can be thankful for forgiveness of sins. God then issued a plea for help in ministry to Isaiah in verse 8: "Then I heard the voice of the Lord saying, 'Whom shall I send? And who will go for us?' "
- *Supplication:* Isaiah expresses his desire in verse 8, "And I said, 'Here am I. Send me!' " A prayer example could be, "Lord, I am willing to be in service for You. I hear Your call on my heart. Fill me with Your Holy Spirit and guide me day by day." God accepts Isaiah's desire and sent him out to share with others in verse 9, "He said, 'Go and tell this people.' "

Yes, let's go and share Jesus with the world!

Get ready

Oh my, look at that smoke plume! That's unusual, I thought. It was September 2020, and I was driving home from work as I pulled over onto the shoulder to watch the smoke plume. A few days earlier there were fires farther south that caused many people to have to leave their

Prayer Still Moves Mountains

homes. Now this new fire was much closer, and it grew steadily. It destroyed homes and vegetation as it moved closer and closer to us. The next day the smoke engulfed us, and the air was an ominous and eerie shade of yellow, and very hazardous to health. The smoke was so thick that Ron and I couldn't see across our yard.

I slowly made my way to work, and thankful to find a room away from the smoke, I stepped inside to inhale deeply before going into the office, where smoke had seeped in through the windows. I never want to take fresh air for granted again!

The area map was divided into three levels of evacuation: Get Ready. Be Set. Go. But for many people the fire came so quickly they were suddenly at the Go level and had to leave immediately—leaving everything behind.

When my road entered the Get Ready level, I was at my mom's house. I called Ron, who said, "I am going through each room of the house, grabbing items we might need and setting them at the entrance to that room. Then if we go to the Be Set level, we will grab those items and put them in the truck. And if we get to the Go level, we'll be ready to go."

Meanwhile, I asked my mom to pack some items in case she also needed to leave. This seemed surreal to me. *Is this really happening?* I wondered. Thankfully, our road never moved beyond the Get Ready level. But we were ready—just in case.

This experience reminded me of the importance of paying attention to Jesus' guidance. The fires were a great example of how we should likewise be in the Get Ready mode for Jesus' coming. He, too, is coming unexpectedly, "So you also must be ready, because the Son of Man will come at an hour you do not expect him" (Matthew 24:44). Jesus' words are like a warning to Be Set for immediate evacuation. And John 14:1–3 shares we need not be troubled. Jesus will return for us. Thankfully, we won't have to pack bags. Jesus already has everything we will need. Let's be ready to leave when we hear Jesus' call, "Let's go!" Philippians 3:20 encourages, "But our citizenship is in heaven. And we eagerly await a Savior from there, the Lord Jesus Christ."

Prayer Still Moves Mountains

Some of my prayer requests have not yet been answered—they are still outstanding, and may be until Jesus returns. Even so, the stories like the ones I share in this book remind me that God is not finished yet. He is working on all the loose ends. Yes, we face chaotic times, but we know that chaos is where "God moments" still happen. We can trust in His work and run to Him who is our strong tower and He will be with us. May God guide us all as we pray and work together in unity for His soon coming kingdom.

He is eager to come get us and share all of eternity together. While we have just a short wait left, we know He helps us with many messages of encouragement in the Bible. One of my mom's favorite verses is Deuteronomy 31:8, "The Lord himself goes before you and will be with you; he will never leave you nor forsake you. Do not be afraid; do not be discouraged." And I hold on to this promise in Revelation 22:20, 21, "He who testifies to these things says, 'Yes, I am coming soon.' Amen, Come, Lord Jesus. The grace of the Lord Jesus be with God's people. Amen."

May God bless us.

Reflection

1. Where in your life do you see the guiding principle of the Lord as your strong tower?

2. If you saw the vision Isaiah saw of the Lord seated on a throne, what would you tell your friends about the experience?

3. Are you able to recall times in your life where God has worked?

4. Take a few moments to thank God and ask for continued blessings till He comes.

5. Get Ready. Be Set. Go. How will you answer Jesus' plea to be ready to go?